An Outline History of Rock and Roll
Third Edition

Randall Snyder

University of Nebraska

KENDALL/HUNT PUBLISHING COMPANY
4050 Westmark Drive   Dubuque, Iowa 52002

From *Howl* by Alan Ginsberg. Copyright © 1956 by Alan Ginsberg. Reprinted by permission.

Copyright © 1996, 1997, 2001 by Randall Snyder

ISBN 0-7872-7703-7

Kendall/Hunt Publishing Company has the exclusive rights to reproduce this work,
to prepare derivative works from this work, to publicly distribute this work,
to publicly perform this work and to publicly display this work.

All rights reserved. No part of this publication may be reproduced,
stored in a retrieval system, or transmitted, in any form or by any
means, electronic, mechanical, photocopying, recording, or otherwise,
without the prior written permission of Kendall/Hunt Publishing Company.

Printed in the United States of America
10 9 8 7 6 5 4 3 2 1

CONTENTS

ACKNOWLEDGEMENT

This book is a practical overview of Rock music and not intended as a work of historical scholarship. For further research the reader is encouraged to pursue more detailed sources, some of which are included in the bibliography in the back of the book. The strategy of this text grew out of teaching a survey course for general students at the University of Nebraska. I would like to thank the University of Nebraska-Lincoln School of Music and its chairman, Lawrence Mallett, for supporting my efforts in establishing this course. Among several students who have contributed to my knowledge of Rock, I would especially like to thank Betheny Vesely, Christian Erickson and Jon Jamison. I am particularly indebted to fellow colleagues Tom Larson and Scott Anderson, and Kent Wolgamott, entertainment writer for the Lincoln Journal Star for their advice and insights.

INTRODUCTION

Focus of Study

Rock music is studied in two distinct contexts:

1. **Aesthetic**: Rock as a sonic artifact, analysis of musical characteristics, including:
   - historical and artistic evolution
   - innovative contributions of individual artists
   - effect of commercialization and technology
   - role of media (radio–film–TV–internet)
   - interrelationship with other arts, especially poetry and film
2. **Societal**: Rock in relation to a wider context with its social and psychological impact:
   - rock as counter cultural defiance of status quo
   - importance of lyrics
   - encouragement of deviant behavior (*sex, drugs, and Rock & Roll*)
   - establishment reaction through censorship
   - political involvement

While some may argue the relative artistic merit of some Rock, there is no question as to Rock's impact on contemporary culture. Rock, along with film, has become the most influential art of the 20th century.

Rock Evolution

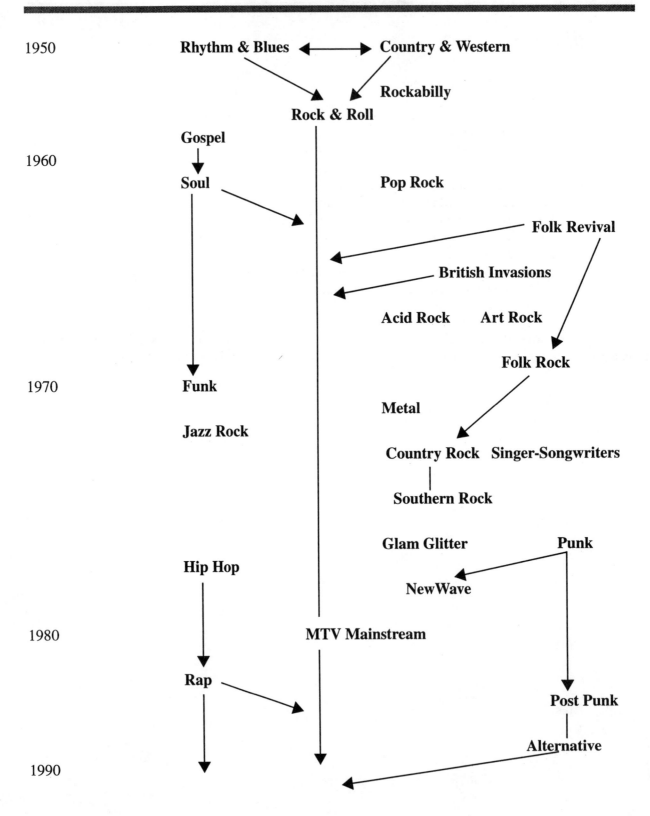

1950   Rhythm & Blues ⟷ Country & Western

Rockabilly

Rock & Roll

Gospel

1960   Soul   Pop Rock

Folk Revival

British Invasions

Acid Rock   Art Rock

Folk Rock

Metal

1970   Funk

Jazz Rock   Country Rock   Singer-Songwriters

Southern Rock

Glam Glitter   Punk

Hip Hop   NewWave

1980   MTV Mainstream

Rap   Post Punk

Alternative

1990

From its beginnings in the 1950s Rock music has evolved through many diverse styles incorporating an ever increasingly complex array of musical techniques. Through its popularity and textual content Rock has had a direct impact on social and political events of the second half of the 20th century.

Some basic themes that remain consistent in this evolution:

1. Black vs. White musical styles and aesthetic
2. growing technological sophistication, especially with recording techniques
3. pendulum swings from complex to simple, abstract to concrete, commercial to return to roots (back to the blues)
4. emphasis on rhythm and a solid sense of pulse
5. importance of the Electric Guitar and bass
6. most important rock has been created by youthful anti-establishment musicians maintaining an alternative, counter-culture stance, often using music as a political statement
7. periodic negative reactions from the Establishment
8. mutual cross fertilization between USA and Britain

While historians may disagree over some of the stylistic subdivisions, the following is a chronological listing of the principle styles of Rock music with important buzz-words used in this class:

1. **Rhythm & Blues**: derived from earlier blues and gospel, R&B represents the African-American roots of Rock and has provided material for all subsequent rock styles (Fats Domino, Little Richard, Chuck Berry, Ray Charles, Bo Diddley)
2. **Rockabilly**: derived from country and R&B: represents the Anglo-American ingredient in early rock (Buddy Holly, Elvis, Jerry Lee Lewis, Carl Perkins)
3. **Rock&Roll**: A classic phase, extending from 1954-1959, White performers combined elements of R&B with Rockabilly to reach a large crossover audience.
4. **Pop Rock**: era of **teen idols** represented White corporate America's reaction to R&R. Includes California Surf (Beach Boys)
5. **Soul**: the commercial evolution of Gospel and R&B became the principle form of Black music in the 1960s (Mo-Town and STAX)
6. **British Invasion**: Mid 1960's rejuvenation by blues-driven Beatles and Rolling Stones, Eric Clapton
7. **Art Rock**: Experimentation with multi-media, electronics and Symphony Orchestras (The Who, Pink Floyd, Frank Zappa)
8. **Psychedelic (Acid)**: mid-late 1960's free-form, drug related music of hippies emanated from California (Jefferson Airplane, Grateful Dead, Doors, Hendrix, Janis Joplin)
9. **Country/Southern**: conservative reaction, emphasis on more traditional (Byrds, Crosby Stills & Nash, Allman Brothers, Lynyrd Skynyrd, ZZ Top)
10. **Folk Rock** and **Singer-Songwriters**: personal often acoustic statements (Dylan, Joni Mitchell, Carole King, Van Morrison, Simon and Garfunkel)
11. **Hard Rock/Heavy Metal**: early 1970s aggressive blues-based guitar-dominated music (Led Zeppelin, Black Sabbath) evolved to speed metal in 1980's (Van Halen, Metallica)
12. **Funk**: Bass guitar driven black ecstatic trance music evolved from Soul (James Brown, Sly, George Clinton) connected with Jazz-Rock (Miles Davis, Herbie Hancock)
13. **Glam/Glitter**: emphasis on visual theatrical use of sets, costumes using lavish stage presentations (Alice Cooper, David Bowie)
14. **Punk**: primitive anti-establishment reaction to Glam (Sex Pistols, The Clash) later evolved into more mainstream **New Wave** (Talking Heads, Police, Devo)
15. 1980s **Mainstream**: commercially oriented superstars: Bruce Springsteen, Madonna, Michael Jackson, **Disco** and **MTV**, influence of **World Music**

16. **Rap**: rhythmic narrative African-American urban music (aka **Hip Hop**) influenced by Jamaican **Reggae** (Run DMC, Two Live Crew, N.W.A.)
17. **Alternative**: catch-all term including post-punk inspired **Grunge**, Industrial, Rave (Nirvana, Pearl Jam, Phish, R.E.M., Sonic Youth)

Origins of Rock & Roll

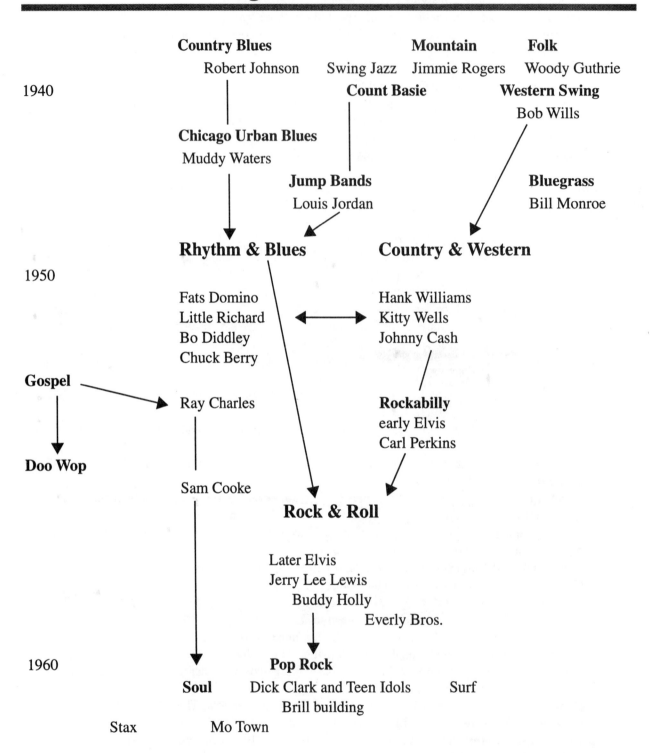

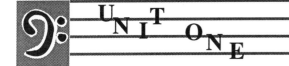

Black Roots

Little Richard, 1956. UPI/CORBIS-BETTMANN.

The Primacy of the Blues

Blues is the most important ingredient in 20th century popular music, especially Rock & Roll. With its direct communication of emotion, visceral rhythmic energy and rich vocal and instrumental nuance, Blues continues to serve as the standard of undiluted honesty from which other musical styles are compared. A myriad of blues-related forms reflecting various degrees of fusion has left its mark on Jazz, Country, and Pop music as well as Rock. The following diagram suggests the continuous evolution of Blues-derived styles.

Blues and Blues-Derived Styles

Timeline: 1900 — 1910 — 1920 — 1930 — 1940 — 1950 — 1960 — 1970

(White Blues)
Hillbilly: Jimmie Rogers   Country & Western: Hank Williams   Country and Southern Rock
Western Swing: Bob Wills   Bluegrass: Bill Monroe   Allman Bros.

(Jazz Blues)
Be-Bop: Bird   Hard Bop Funk: Horace Silver
Monk   Cannonball Adderley

Acid Rock: Jimi Hendrix
Janis Joplin

Kansas City Shouters : Walter Brown
Joe Turner

Boogie-Woogie: Meade Lux Lewis
solo piano   Jay McShann

Rockabilly - **Rock & Roll**
Bill Haley   Buddy Holly
Elvis   Jerry Lee Lewis

Fats Domino
Rhythm & Blues Louis Jordan   Chuck Berry   British Blues: Stones
dance swing rhythms, sax solo   Little Richard   Eric Clapton
party music   Bo Diddley

(Gospel Pop Blues)

Soul   Ray Charles   MoTown: Gladys Knight   **Funk**
Gospel, call & response ,shouting   STAX: Wilson Pickett   Sly Stone
Aretha Franklin
James Brown

(Mainstream Blues)
Country Blues   **Urban Blues**
solo, acoustic, free forms   *amplified guitar, drums, harmonica*
regional styles
Delta: Bukka White   Memphis: B.B. King
Robert Johnson   Albert King

Classic Blues
standard forms , female singers
piano, jazz combo
W.C. Handy
Bessie Smith
Louis Armstrong

Chicago: Sonny Boy Williamson
Elmore James
Texas: Blind Lemmon Jefferson   Willie Dixon
Lightnin' Hopkins   Albert Collins
Muddy Waters   Magic Slim

Eastern: Sonny Terry
Brownnie McGhee

sources:
Work Song
Field Holler
Gospel Music

basics:
lyric content
musical form
Blue Notes

Rhythm & Blues: (1940-1954)

Rhythm and Blues (R&B) is the most important precursor to Rock. Begun in the late 1930s, it was referred to as race music until 1949, when Billboard Magazine's classification of R&B was created. Almost exclusively created by African-Americans, it persisted as a distinct musical genre until the early 1960s when it evolved into Soul, the Funk of the 1970s, and Hop Hop of the 1980s.

I. General Characteristics

1. commercial synthesis of Blues, Gospel, Big-band swing, Boogie-Woogie
2. electric bass eventually replaces acoustic bass used in jazz
3. dance music, emphasizing enjoyment of life rather than its problems
4. tenor saxophone principle solo instrument
5. stage choreography and showmanship important
6. R&B was an important social element in segregated Black communities

II. Early History

1. Dave Clark grandfather of R&B
   - became advance man and consultant for Decca, the first promotion man
   - the spread of R&B became linked with Black Radio

2. Jump Bands **Louis Jordan**: began recording for Decca in 1938 with the Tympany Five (actually seven players). Created a dance style called shuffle boogie or Jump blues. Marketed to both White and Black audiences, Jordan was an early crossover artist.

3. other Jump Bands included Lionel Hampton

4. **Muddy Waters** (1915-1983) Most influential of Chicago Bluesmen, Waters' recordings in the early 1950s at Chess help define the new electric Urban Blues sound
   - b. McKinley Morganfield in Rolling Fork, Mississippi. Influenced by Son House and Robert Johnson
   - moved to Chicago, 1943, began recording in 1947.
   - most influential band included Little Richard, harmonica, Otis Spann, piano, Jimmy Rogers, guitar
   - important hits include:
     * *I'm Your Hoochie Coochie Man* (1953)
     * *Got My Mojo Working* (1956)
   - influential tour of England, 1958

5. Chicago became important center of R&B. Some influential blues artists included:
   - Big Bill Broonzy (1893-1958) link between country and urban styles
   - Sonny Boy Williamson (1988-1965) toured Britain and recorded with the Yardbirds
   - John Lee Hooker (1917-) recorded into the 1980s and featured in *The Blues Brothers*
   - Elmore James (1918-1963) slide guitar approach influenced Eric Clapton
   - Willie Dixon (1915-1992) tunes covered by Led Zeppelin
   - Howlin' Wolf (1926 -) came to Chicago from Memphis

6. Jackie Brenston and Ike Turner's *Rocket 88* with its Boogie-Woogie bass and story line became a prototype for 1950s Rock & Roll

III. Early Independent Recording Companies (Indies) At first the major recording companies (Columbia, RCA) refused to record black music and most R&B were recorded at small independent studios, some of the more important include:

- Specialty 1946, Los Angeles (owner, Art Rupe), Little Richard
- **Atlantic** 1947, New York, (Ahmet Ertegun), Drifters, Joe Turner, Ray Charles
- **Chess** 1947, Chicago, (Chess Bros). specialized at first in Blues, Muddy Waters, later Bo Diddley, Chuck Berry, Etta James
- Peacock 1949, Houston (Don Robey), Little Richard, Johnny Ace
- Imperial 1949 (Lew Chudd) Los Angeles
- Trumpet 1950 Jackson Miss. (Willard And Lillian McMurry) Elmore James and Sonny Boy Williamson
- **Sun** 1952 Memphis (Sam Phillips) Elvis, Jerry Lee Lewis, Carl Perkins
- Vee-Jay 1952, Chicago, Gary (James and Vivian Bracken), The Impressions, early Beatles

IV. Black Radio was an important force in the segregated community besides disseminating R&B to crossover audiences, Radio:

- helped black businesses reach potential buyers
- named shops where blacks could enter without fear of harassment
- provided prestigious jobs for blacks
- provided outlet for community service announcements by Civic and Church
- exposed R&B to white audiences

1. Important Deejays;
   - Jack Cooper, began broadcasting The Negro Hour in Chicago by 1935
   - Al Benson (The Midnight Gambler) Chicago spoke in vernacular
   - Lavada Durst (Dr. Hep Cat) Austin and Jocko Henderson, NY, spoke in Bop scatology.
   - Jack Gibson started first black-owned station WERD in Atlanta, 1949
   - Hot Rod Hulbert WDIA Memphis (The Mother Station of the Negroes) where B.B.King got his start
   - Dr. Daddy-O New Orleans

2. Payola: payment to DJs by artists to plug their songs was an integral part of the business. Later, (1958) the major labels will use payola as an attack on the indies.

R&B to Rock and Roll (1950s)

By the 1950s R&B had become noticed by young white audiences and many performers became crossover superstars. R&B evolved into Rock and Roll.

I. Important Performers:

1. **Fats Domino** (Antoine Domino b. New Orleans 1929-) pianist, singer
   - smooth, relaxed vocal style and non-confrontational persona gave Domino wide crossover appeal, sold 65 million records
   - piano style used Boogie-Woogie bass lines
   - began recording in 1950 (Imperial) important recordings (with Dave Bartholomew arrangements, and Cosimo Matassa, studio engineer) include:
     - *Ain't That A Shame* 1955
     - *Blueberry Hill* 1956
     - *I'm Walkin* 1956
     - *Walking to New Orleans* 1960

2. **Bo Diddley** (Ellas Danielson 1928-) singer, guitarist, born MS, moved to Chicago
    -   raw, "primitive" style
    -   uses blues guitar techniques (bottle neck, glissandi)
    -   repetitive rhythms (Bo Diddley beat) derived from Afro-Cuban tradition
    -   important recordings with Chess:
        •   *Bo Diddley* 1955
        •   *Who Do You Love* 1956

Bo Diddley © Neal Preston/CORBIS

3. **Little Richard** (b. Richard Penniman, Macon, Ga. 1935-) pianist, singer
    -   used gospel effects (shrieks and moans, high energy, fast tempos)
    -   androgynous stage appearance
    -   began recording in 1951 (RCA Peacock), first hit *Tutti Frutti* 1955 (Specialty) ("A Wop Bop Alu Bop, A Wop Bam Boom Aw Rooty")
    -   1957-1964 retired from music and joined ministry. After comeback never achieved prior success. Other important recordings:
        •   *Long Tall Sally* 1956
        •   *Good Golly Miss Molly* released 1958
        •   *Ready Teddy*
4. **Chuck Berry** (b. St. Louis 1926-) guitarist, composer, enjoyed crossover success by consciously combining elements of country with R&B

- wrote sophisticated, humorous, non-sentimental lyrics on teen themes
- added country two beat with R&B backbeat
- transferred piano boogie-woogie to guitar with trademark two note chords
- combined traditional 12-bar blues form with 8-bar verses
- important recordings with Chess begin 1955:
    - *Maybelline* 1955 reached #5 on Pop charts, first hit for Chess, mixes blues with verse forms
    - *Roll Over Beethoven* 1956
    - *School Day* 1957
    - *Johnny B. Goode* 1958 opens with classic syncopated guitar solo
    - *Nadine* 1964
- imprisoned (after two trials) from 1959-1964 on violation of Mann Act.

5. **Ray Charles** (Ray Charles Robinson 1930-) pianist, singer. Born, Albany, Ga., raised in Florida, listened to variety of music
    - important assimilator of Gospel with R&B with exuberance, falsetto, raspy vocal style, call and response, major influence of Soul
    - developed glaucoma, lost sight at age 6, cut first record 1949
    - signed with Atlantic 1952
        - *Jumpin' in the Morning* 1952: Jump Style
    - recorded in New Orleans with Dave Bartholomew 1953
    - landmark recording *I Got A Woman* 1955 introduces gospel
    - added gospel trio Raelettes with hit recordings
        - *I'm Movin On* 1959: mix of country/R&B
        - *What'd I Say* 1959: use of Wurlitzer el.pf. and call and response
    - began to incorporate pop and country elements with:
        - *Georgia On My Mind* 1960
        - *I Can't Stop Loving You* 1962 (sold 3 million)

6. **Sam Cooke** (1935-1964) singer
    - light, high range combined pop with gospel
    - became black teen idol. Shot to death in 1964
    - hit recording:
        - *You Send Me* 1957

II. **Doo-Wop**: vocal quartet with use of wordless (scat) singing and falsetto obligato above melody, speaking bass. Use of triplet subdivision in piano and "doo wop progression".

- influenced by Mills Bros., Ink Spots, and gospel quartets
  important recordings (often one-time hits):
    - 1949 *Tell Me So* The Ravens, began using wordless falsetto
    - 1953 *Crying in the Chapel* The Orioles, country cover
    - 1954 *Sh-Boom* The Chords
    - 1954 *Earth Angel* The Penguins, #1 R&B hit
    - 1958 *Get A Job* Silhouettes
    - 1958 *Book Of Love* The Monotones
  important longer-lasting groups:
    - The Platters used more complex jazz harmonies: *Smoke Gets In Your Eyes*
    - The Coasters: *Young Blood*
    - **The Drifters** (with Clyde McPhatter, lead singer) added latin rhythms
    - *Spanish Harlem, On Broadway*

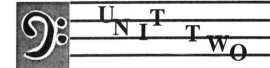

White Roots

Jimmie Rodgers, 1929. FRANK DRIGGS/CORBIS-BETTMANN.

Anglo-American Folk Music

The Anglo-American forms of music that directly influenced Rock & Roll evolved out of earlier traditional folk music.

I.   Some General Characteristics

1.   evolved from English ballad tradition preserved in the Appalachian region
2.   acoustic Instruments, including the fiddle, dulcimer and autoharp

3.   solo or small ensemble
4.   straight forward singing style often high-pitched and nasal with little vibrato
5.   non-commercial non-professional performers
6.   social and left wing political agendas

II. The Importance of John (1872-1948) and Alan Lomax (1915-)

This father and son team of musicologists helped preserve Anglo-American folk music through field recordings and publication. Their research, including Appalachian and Southern African-American blues and gospel music, also provided repertoire for later singers.

Regional Folk Song Style Areas According to Lomax

1.   The North: includes the New England and Middle Atlantic States, and the area between the Ohio river and the Great Lakes
     -   singing characterized by hard, clear tone
     -   less puritanical than the South, women more independent

2.   The Southern Mountains and Backwoods: includes the marginal land of "poor white" populations, especially in Western North Carolina, Kentucky and Tennessee
     -   geographical isolation responsible for survival of British folk styles well into the 20th century
     -   high-pitches and nasal singing style became model for subsequent commerical Country & Western
     -   strong fundamentalist Protestant ethic ("Bible Belt")

3.   Ozarks: transitional area including parts of Missouri and Arkansas combining Northern and Southern traits
     -   developed distinct fiddling style

4.   The West: created genres of cowboy ballads and outlaw songs
     -   home of Western Swing

III. Influential performers:

Woody Guthrie © Bettmann/CORBIS

1. **Woody Guthrie** (1912-1967) championed the plight of the migrants, Union workers, directly influenced Bob Dylan. Wrote *This Land Is Your Land*, anthem of the 1960s.
   - autobiography *Bound for Glory*
2. **Pete Seeger** (1919-) sang songs researched by his musicologist father, Charles (1886-1979)
3. Burl Ives (1900-) through TV and film became the most visible folk singer
4. two ensembles: The Almanac Singers: formed in 1941 by Seeger, and The Weavers, formed in 1948, (blacklisted in the 1950s) updated traditional songs with politically relevant texts.

(The important role folk music had in revitalizing Rock in the 1960s will be discussed in Unit VI)

Country Music (1930-1950)

Beginning around 1930, various forms of Anglo-American music began to be recorded that were to have an important influence on the Rock and Roll of the 1950s. These included a commercial form of string band dance music from Appalachia that later became known as Country (or Country & Western), and Bluegrass, which emphasized instrumental virtuosity.

History of Country Music

I. Hillbilly (or Mountain) Music

1. extensive recording began in Bristol, Tennessee, 1927 with amateur bands

typical ensemble: **String Band**, fiddle (violin), banjo, guitar, later mandolin, string bass

2. family bands included the Carter Family (Maybelle, A.P., and Sara), popularized autoharp
3. **Jimmie Rodgers** ("The Singing Brakeman") recorded 1927-1933 (RCA) sold over 20 million records.
   - sang blues and recorded with Black musicians
4. **Grand Ole Opry** opened in Nashville 1925, beginning of live broadcasting
   - later WLS National Barn Dance (Chicago) KWKH Louisiana Hayride (Shreveport)

II. **Bluegrass**: developed after 1945 represented a modernized, professional expression of the String Band tradition, Emphasized virtuosic instrumental playing, three finger banjo pickin' style introduced by Scruggs.

1. Bill Monroe's Blue Grass Boys began in 1938. 1945 added **Lester Flatt**, guitar, and **Earl Scruggs**, banjo
2. 1948 Scruggs and Flatt start their own classic band.
3. "New Grass" a later style used elements of C&W and Rock

Bluegrass String Band Usage

- Violin (fiddle): primary melodic instrument, combined Mountain drones with Western Swing and some Jazz techniques
- Banjo: virtuosic three finger arpeggiation style introduced by Earl Scruggs around 1945
- Mandolin: used both as harmony rhythm and secondary melody behind fiddle
- Guitar: primarily rhythm instrument with strings usually left to vibrate, some melodic runs on lower strings

III. **Black-influenced Country Styles**: Influenced by recordings of Jazz and R&B bands and individuals developed hybrid styles in the 1940s.

1. **Western Swing**: Fiddler Bob Wills (1905-1976) and The Texas Playboys used jazz improvisation with Country
   - broadcast 1934-1942 at KVOO, Tulsa, Ok. *San Antonio Rose*, biggest hit
2. Hillbilly Boogie: groups like the Delmore Bros., direct precursor to Rockabilly
3. Honky-Tonk (refers to saloon): Ernest Tubb and Fred Tillman

IV. **Country & Western**: represented a commercial blend of the popular music of crooners such as Bing Crosby with Hillbilly that differed from Bluegrass in that it used electric instruments, steel guitar and drums and emphasized vocals telling personal stories over instrumentals. Female vocalists became important. Nashville became the recording center for C&W. The Western element was influenced by the singing cowboys Gene Autry, Tex Ritter, and Roy Rogers.

Hank Williams C&W's first superstar
Consummate composer with simple, direct lyrics, Williams, who became known as the "Hillbilly Shakespeare", was the first Country artist who appealed to teens as well as adults. Many of his tunes transcended Country and were covered by Pop singers.

1. b. 1923, Georgiano, Alabama
   - influenced by Blues musician age 7
   - started singing professionally at age 13 with "The Drifting Cowboys"
   - achieved success of Louisiana Hayride but fired from Grand 'Ole Opry in 1952 for singing *Lovesick Blues*

2. Recordings: wrote 125 songs beginning in 1946, first on Stirling label, then MGM.
    Some important hits:
    - *Lovesick Blues* 1949
    - *Cold, Cold Heart Blues* 1951 (covered by Tony Bennet in 1951)
    - *Hey Good Lookin'* 1951
    - *Your Cheatin' Heart* 1952
    - *Jambala* 1952
3. Career shortened by alcoholism. Died Jan. 1, 1954 in the back seat of a Cadillac on way to a gig.

Comparison with Elvis

Hank Williams was a great influence on Elvis Presley, and they had much in common. Both came from poor White, Southern backgrounds and later acquired a taste for flashy clothes. Both blended C&W with blues. Some differences between the two included the fact that Elvis was not a composer, and had a more virtuosic voice than Williams', using more Blues and Gospel elements.

4. Important female vocalists:
    - Kitty Wells
    - Patsy Cline
    - Loretta Lynn
5. Important **Nashville** session players included:
    - Chet Atkins, guitar
    - Floyd Cramer, piano
    - Roy Acuff, fiddle

(The important merger of Country and Rock in the 1960s will be discussed in Unit Nine)

Comparison between Country and Rhythm & Blues

While much diversity exists within Country music and Rhythm & Blues, the following is a comparison of the most common elements:

	Country	Rhythm & Blues
1.	Emphasis on steady precise beat	Melodies play off beat (syncopated)
2.	Slow to moderate tempos	Often faster, exuberant tempos
3.	Acoustic bass plays in 4/4 on 1 and 3	More active electric bass plays on all beats or twice on every beat (boogie woogie)
4.	Harmony simple chords	Blue Chords using added 7th
5.	Personal lyrics dealing with sad love	Same, except more explicit sexual affairs or loneliness imagery. Urban themes
6.	Political topics (in Folk)	Generally absent, or veiled in metaphor
7.	Nasal, non vibrato vocal sound	Full-voice, vibrato reflecting gospel bkg
8.	Soft, retrained volume	Loud, aggressive volume
9.	Violin, steel guitar	Tenor saxophone
10.	Banjo, chordally strumed acoustic guitar	linear style electric guitar
11.	Minimal drums	Strong drum presence

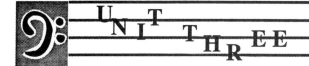

White Rock and Roll (1954-1959)

Elvis Presley, 1956. UPI/CORBIS-BETTMANN.

By the early 1950s, a proto-rock music combining aspects of Rhythm & Blues and Country began reaching a large audience comprised of white, middle class, suburban teenagers. The classic phase of Rock & Roll began with the Rockabilly recordings of Elvis Presley at Sam Phillips' Sun Studios in Memphis and dominated the charts until 1959, when a smoother pop style took over.

Social Trends

I. Teenage Suburbia: ("nothing to do, nowhere to go")

1. youth (ages 14-24) culture previously dictated by parents, school, police
   - safe parentally-sponsored activity (sports and arts) not for everyone
   - in the 1950s for the first time a true teenage culture was created
2. lack of public transportation made cars (with radios) essential
3. suburban crime (loitering, vandalism, petty larceny, public intoxication) random resistance to boredom
4. "Generation Gap": the rise of the juvenile delinquent: "Sex, drugs, and Rock & Roll" (and food and clothes and gangs)

II. Rise of teen consumer power: In 1956 there were 13 million teenagers in America with an income of $7 billion a year with an average weekly allowance of $10.55. The average teen bought from 2 to 12 records a month.

1. between 1953-1959 record sales increased from $213 to $603 million, mostly 45s through sales of Rock to teenage girls
2. advertising catered to teens: age of fads (Hula Hoop, Coonskin Caps etc.)
3. availability of cheap radios: transistor radios marketed in 1958

III. Seminal Films: films as well as music shaped teen attitudes.

1. **Marlon Brando** in *The Wild One* 1954 ("What are you rebelling against? Whaddya got?")
2. **James Dean** in *Rebel Without A Cause* 1955
3. **Blackboard Jungle** with main-title music by Bill Haley and the Comets

IV. Growing importance of DJs

1. **Alan Freed** (1922-1965)
   - 1951 WJW Cleveland: began playing R&B to White audience on Moondog Show
   - 1952: began promoted first Rock concert which through overbooking led to first riot
   - 1954: moved to New York, and 6-night a week 11:00 PM-2:00 AM show called **Rock and Roll** Show (unsuccessfully tried to copyright term)
   - 1958 Boston: police force cancellation of show charging Freed with anarchy and incitement to riot (Freed: "Hey kids, the cops don't want you to have a good time")
   - 1962: Freed found guilty in Payola Scandal and tax evasion
2. Other important White DJs:
   • Symphony Sid Torin (NY)
   • Daddy-O-Daylie (Chicago)
   • Wolfman Jack (Shreveport)
   • Jean Shepherd (NY)
   • Murray the K (NY)
   • Dewey Phillips (Memphis)

Rockabilly (1954-1956)

I. General Characteristics

1. music of high spirits and youthful rebellion created primarily by poor white, southern males

2. nervous, fast tempos
3. standard instrumentation:
   - lead electric guitar
   - acoustic rhythm guitar
   - string bass
   - drums (at first, optional)
4. backbeats, and slapping bass
5. hiccups, stutters and vibrato vocal effects enhanced by studio echo

II. Bill Haley (1925-1981)

1. DJ turned Country singer with the Saddlemen, changed named to the Comets in 1952 and covered *Rocket 88*
2. 1954 records **Rock Around The Clock** (Decca), used as main-title music for *Blackboard Jungle* 1955, sold 3 million
   - other hits: *Shake, Rattle, and Roll*, covered Joe Turner, *See Ya Later, Alligator*
3. toured Britain in 1957 becoming first international rock star
4. Starred in 1957 film *Rock Around the Clock*, with Alan Freed and Little Richard

III. Importance of Sam Phillips and Sun Studios

1. saw the economic potential of Rockabilly's synthesis ("I could make a million dollars if I could find a white man that could sing like a black")
2. founded Sun Studios 1952: first hit *Rocket 88* (released on Chess), by Jackie Benson and Ike Turner. Also recorded B.B. King, Howlin' Wolf, and the Prisonaires "Walking in the Rain" 1953
3. Recorded Elvis (1954-1955) Jerry Lee Lewis (23 records) Carl Perkins (1954-1958) Johnny Cash, Roy Orbison
4. recording techniques: echo
5. Sun closed in 1963. Phillips became major shareholder with Holiday Inn

Elvis Presley

Unquestionably the pivotal figure of rock, Elvis, in his early recordings defined Rock & Roll's musical style as well its social context of teenage rebellion.

I. Brief bio:

1. b. Tupelo, Miss. 1935, into lower class poor white family
   brought up member of Pentecostal First Assembly of God
   began playing guitar at age 11, listened to Jimmie Rodgers and Muddy Waters
2. moved to Memphis, 1948 and absorbed Beale St. blues
   graduated from High School in 1953 and became a truck driver
3. meteoric rise to fame:
   - July 1954 records *That's All Right Mama/Blue Moon of Kentucky* with guitarist Scotty Moore and Bill Black, string bass
   - Aug. 1954 first professional gig, Sept. Grand Ole Opry
   - July 1955 released *Mystery Train*, first #1 hit
   - Oct. 1956 culmination of TV appearances on Jackie Gleason, Milton Berle, Steve Allen and Ed Sullivan Show (from the waist up)
4. Colonel Tom Parker became manager and signs with RCA
   records string of hits:

- *Heartbreak Hotel* 1956
- *Blue Suede Shoes*
- *Don't Be Cruel/Hound Dog*
- *Love Me Tender*
- *All Shook Up*

5. made first movie *Love Me Tender*, followed by *Loving You* and *Jailhouse Rock* 1957
6. drafted in army 1958-1960 in Germany, returned to film and pop song
7. 1969 staged rock & roll comeback
8. died Aug. 16, 1977 of heart disease

II. Musical Characteristics: combined C&W and R&B traditions

1. wide range of vocal styles: gospel, blues, country, pop
2. virtuosic command of vocal techniques (stutters, hiccups etc.)
3. made stage choreography important part of rock performance

Buddy Holly

In a short career that spanned just two years, Buddy Holly became one of Rock's most important composers with songs that synthesized diverse styles of country, Western Swing, blues, R&B, and even some Latin elements.

I. Bio:

1. b. Charles Holley, 1936, in Lubbock, Texas. Secure childhood opposite of R&R rebel stereotype
2. formed Western Swing band in high school, met Elvis and worked as back-up band for Bill Haley
3. first unsuccessful country recordings in Nashville with Decca 1956
    - *Rock Around With Ollie Vee Elvis* influenced
4. formed the Crickets 1957 (Jerry Allison, drums, Joe Mauldin, bass, Niki Sullivan, rhythm guitar) recorded 7 top 10 hits at Clovis, N.M. produced by Norman Petty including:
    - *That'll Be The Day*   first and most popular release
    - *Peggy Sue*
    - *Words of Love*   example of overdubbing
    - *Oh Boy* rockabilly style
    - *Not Fade Away* uses "Bo Diddley" beat played on cardboard box
    - *Maybe Baby* country style
    - *Well All Right* Latin tinged folk rock
    - *It's So Easy*
    - *Every Day* Celeste intro
5. played Apollo Theater; tours of Britain, Australia
6. after breakup with the Crickets, moved to New York, began writing for Paul Anka, et al
    - *It Doesn't Matter Anymore* with strings
    - *True Love Ways*
7. died in plane crash 1959 ("the day the music died") age 22
    - *Peggy Sue Got Married* posthumous release

II. Musical Characteristics: unique singer, composer, guitarist, producer

1. composer of innocent, childlike love songs
2. light vocal style, with hiccups and sudden glisses
3. helped popularize the **Fender Stratocaster** solid body electric guitar

4. used overdubbing and multi-track recording techniques, especially vocal backgrounds
5. Crickets instrumentation became standard rock combo for next decade - direct influence on Beatles, Rolling Stones, The Hollies, etc.

Other Important Performers

1. **Jerry Lee Lewis** (1935-) pianist, singer
   - b. Ferriday, LA. rebellious youth; grew up listening to honky-tonk piano
   - brash, flamboyant performer (The Killer)
   - frenetic piano style based on simple boogie-woogie with glissandos and triplets
   - career peaked at Steve Allen Show appearance
   - hits recorded at Sun:
     • *Whole Lot Of Shakin' Goin On* 1957
     • *Great Balls Of Fire*
   - career foundered after marriage to 13-year-old third cousin Mona Gale (while still married to second wife)

Jerry Lee Lewis © Bettmann/CORBIS

2. **Johnny Cash** (1932 -) combined emotional directness of C&W with Rockabilly
   - unusual deep baritone voice
     early Sun hits include *Folsom Prison Blues* 1955 and *I Walk The Line* 1956
   - later recorded with Dylan on Nashville Skyline

3. **Carl Perkins** (1932 - 1998) singer, guitarist
   - groomed as Elvis' replacement at Sun
   - *Let The Jukebox Keep On Playing* 1955, shown Hank Williams influence
   - *Blue Suede Shoes* 1956: first tune to chart #1 on both country and R&B charts
   - other songs *Honey, Don't*, 1955 and *Everybody's Tryin' To Be My Baby* 1956 covered by the Beatles
   - career halted by car accident
4. **Everly Bros.** (Don 1937- Phil 1938-) most countrified of rockabilly singers
   - b. Tennessee into family of country musicians
   - recorded string of top 10 hits for Cadence in Nashville featuring Appalachian-style high tenor duet harmony in 3rds, accompanied by string band with Chet Atkins, guitar, and Floyd Cramer, piano, music composed by Boudleaux and Felice Bryant:
     - *Bye Bye Love* 1957 with Chet Atkins
     - *Wake Up Little Suzie* 1957
     - *All I Have To Do Is Dream* 1958
   - joined Warner Bros. with biggest hit:
     - *Cathy's Clown* 1960

The Decline of Rock and Roll

I. Near the end of the 1950s, several factors led to the decline of Rock & Roll:

1. deaths of Buddy Holly, Richie Valens and The Big Bopper in plane crash near Fargo, ND, Feb. 3, 1959
2. conviction of Chuck Berry for violation of Mann Act
3. damage to Jerry Lee Lewis' career after marriage to cousin
4. Elvis' induction in the army
5. retirement of Little Richard from music
6. injury to Carl Perkins

II. Growing opposition from church, civic, and corporate America:

- 1955 *Encyclopedia Britannica*: The rock'roll school in general concentrated on a minimum of melodic line and a maximum of rhythmic noise, deliberately competing with the artistic ideals of the jungle itself
- *New York Times*: (rock'roll is) ...communicable disease and a ...cannibalistic and tribalistic kind of music
- *White Citizens Council of Birmingham, Alabama*... rock...appealed to the base in man (and) brings out animalism and vulgarity
- *Vance Packard*, author of the *Hidden Persuaders*: rock and roll stirred the animal instinct in modern teenagers with its raw savage tone
- *Frank Sinatra*, testifying before Congress 1958: rock is... the most brutal, ugly, desperate, vicious form of expression it has been my misfortune to hear
- *Meredith Wilson*, composer of *The Music Man*: 'rock and roll is dull, ugly, amateurish, immature, trite, banal, and stale. It glorifies the mediocre, the nasty, the bawdy, the cheap, the tasteless

III. Payola Scandal

Pressured by the conservative ASCAP (which was in competition with BMI) and the major recording companies (RCA, Columbia, Decca), whose sales were threatened by the success of the Indies, the

House Legislative Oversight Committee, chaired by Rep. Oren Harris was formed in 1959 to investigate charges of corrupt broadcasting practices (including TV Quiz shows). As a result of the investigations, several law suits forced some Indies and DJ's (including Alan Freed) out of business.

Postscript: Changes in the Recording Industry

I. **The significance of the 45 rpm** 45's became the most important mode of rock & roll dissemination.

1. introduced with new vinyl composition in 1949 by RCA
2. 1954 new lower-priced players were introduced that could fit conventional spindles
3. during the period 1954-1956 45s surpassed and made the old 78 rpm records obsolete
4. advantages of 45s for teen consumers:
   - cheaper, quicker to manufacture (due to the development of automatic injection and compression systems) and distribute (easier to mail)
   - unbreakable vinyl construction made listening more casual experience
   - 3 minute time frame suitable for teen attention span

II. **33 rpm record** (introduced at about the same time as the 45) with its time frame of 25 minutes per side became associated with adult, serious listeners of classical and pop.

1. originally issued in two formats: seven-inch single (which died out) and the 12 inch LP album
2. Rock's shift to the LP in the 1960s implies the changing nature of Rock's audience
3. LP's made 45s obsolete by mid 1960s

III. Cassette tape

1. first sold in 1963
2. gained in popularity with introduction of portable Walkman player 1981

IV. **Compact Disc**

1. introduced in 1982, widespread by 1988
2. vinyl records become obsolete
3. CDs revitalized the recording industry with nostalgia re-releases

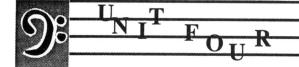

Pop Rock (early 1960s)

The Beach Boys, 1965. UPI/CORBIS-BETTMANN.

Pop music consciously designed for the largest possible audience is usually simple, and meant to be understood easily at first hearing with a memorable phrase, or **hook** (which often contains the title of the song) sung at least twice. Pop Rock of the early 60s was often a bland non-threatening, non-confrontational style that represented a watered-down version of rock & roll and rhythm & blues. The creative center of the music shifted from the performer to the songwriter and producer.

The Folk—Pop—Art Concept

Pop music often incorporates aspects of Folk music to suggest a deeper emotional quality and honesty, while Art, or classical music, is used to suggest more sophistication. Folk elements are sometimes used to target a specific ethnic audience while Art is used for older listeners.

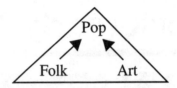

Folk and Pop music have in turn influenced Art music (Post modernism).

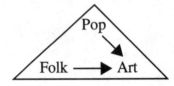

Changes in Recording Techniques

With the availability of the Ampex tape recorder in 1948, recorded music became more and more an artificial product of the recording studio distinct from a live performance (real time). Early recording techniques included:

- sound enhancement (reverb)
- editing through cutting and splicing (double tracking of solo voice)
- multi tracks (from 4 to 24 during the 1960s) allowed for more control over mixing as well as complexity
- sound effects (musique concrete)

Dick Clark and the Importance of American Bandstand

I. Dick Clark (1929-) began national broadcasting of American Bandstand from Philadelphia in 1957. Projected a safe, clean-cut, mostly white image of rock.

   1. launched the careers of several **Teen Idols** whose good looks were often more important than their musicianship:
- Fabian (Fabian Forte 1943-)
- Frankie Avalon (Francis Avallone 1940-) *Venus* #1 hit 1959
- Bobby Rydell (Robert Ridarelli (1942-)

   2. created dance crazes, especially Chubby Checker's the **Twist**

II. Other teen idols (many who became movie stars):

1. Pat Boone (1934) began covering R&B material in mid 1950s
2. Paul Anka (1941-) wrote most of his hit songs
3. Connie Francis (Concetta Franconero 1938-)
4. Ricky Nelson (1940-1985) child actor in parent's TV show

Pat Boone © Hulton-Deutsch Collection/CORBIS

Brill Building Updates Tin Pan Alley

In 1958 Don Kirschner established Aldon Music Co. at 1619 Broadway, across the street from the Brill Building and hired songwriting teams that from 1959-1964 dominated the music industry (with the important exception of Mo-Town). The best of this music combined professional craftsmanship with a direct teenage-oriented message.

I. Important songwriter teams:

1. Gerry Goffin (music)/Carole King (words)
    *   *Hey Girl, Will You Love Me In The Morning*
2. Neil Sedaka/Howie Greenfield
    *   *Breaking Up Is Hard To Do*

3. Barry Mann/Cynthia Weil
   - *Blame It On The Bossa Nova*

II. Other Independent song writing teams:

1. Jerry **Leiber**/Mike **Stoller**: began in Los Angeles in early 1950s to combine R&B with Pop
   - *Hound Dog* 1952 Willie Mae Thornton
   - *Young Blood* 1957 Coasters (formerly the Robins)
   - *Jailhouse Rock* 1957 Elvis
   Later worked for Atlantic:
   - *There Goes My Baby* 1959 Drifters, introduced strings to R&B
   - *Stand By Me* 1961 Ben King
   - *Spanish Harlem* Drifters
2. Bert Bacharach/Hal David

III. Girl Groups: sub-genre of Pop Rock targeted specifically for teenage girls (bubble gum)

1. most performers African-American 16-19 yr old girls
2. lyrics usually about utopian, innocent teenage love (the boy)
3. performers subservient to composers and producers
4. Phil Spector's Wall Of Sound
5. important groups and hits:
   - Shirelles: *Will You Love Me Tomorrow* 1960 first #1 hit by girl group
   - Crystals: *Da Doo Ron Ron* 1963
   - Ronettes: *Be My Baby* 1963
   - Shangri-Las: *Leader Of The Pack* 1964

IV. The importance of **Phil Spector** (1940-): most influential producer of 1960s

1. Helped establish producer as important creative force in recording process - exerted complete control over production
2. **Wall of Sound**: thick instrumental backgrounds inspired by Wagner: "a Wagnerian approach to rock and roll," "little symphonies for the kids"
   - large orchestra with multiple doubling of instruments, percussion (300 musicians used for 1969 "Proud Mary")
   - extensive overdubbing and mixing creating thick and full textures (did not like stereo which separated sounds)
   - use of prerecorded sound effects
   - loud dynamics (meant to be heard on cheap radios)
3. Some important Spector recordings:
   - Teddy Bears 1958: *To Know Him Is To Love Him*
   - Crystals 1962: *He's A Rebel*
   - Ronettes 1963: *Be My Baby*
   - Righteous Bros. 1965: *Unchained Melody*
   - Ike & Tina Turner 1966: ***River Deep-Mountain High***
   - Beatles: *Let It Be, Abbey Road* 1969
   - George Harrison 1970: *All Things Must Pass*

Surf

A West Coast pop music rawer and raunchier than the East Coast style, surf capitalized on the California Myth and popularized the surf culture which represented the first of many counter-culture movement of the

1960s. Its lean, energetic guitar-based sound combined aspects of R&B with pop vocals. The surf craze was also reflected in a string of genre films, such as *Beach Party* 1963, and *Bikini Beach* 1964, starring Frankie Avalon and Annette Funicello. The surf life style, the first dropout culture of the 1960s, spawned its own lexicon of slang that was used in song lyrics (see addenda).

I. **Instrumental Music:** Surf was one of the first styles to feature purely instrumental tunes:

1. **Dick Dale** (Richard Monsour 1937-) The "King of the Surf Guitar" created lexicon of guitar effects, using Fender Stratocaster or Jaguars through Showman amps:
    -   tremolo (fast repeating note) showing Middle Eastern Bouzouki influence: *Misirlou*
    -   rapid glissandos (said to imitate sound of waves)
    -   *Let's Go Tripin'* 1961 sax/guitar feature first Surf hit
2. Duane Eddy and the Ventures
    -   twangy sound created by plucking close to the bridge
    -   bending pitch with tremolo arm
        theme music for *Hawaii Five-O* 1969

II. **Important Surf and Garage Bands**

1. Surfaris: *Wipe Out* 1963
2. Chantays: *Pipeline* 1963
3. Jan & Dean: *Surf City*
4. The Kingsmen (from Portland) ***Louie, Louie*** 1963. Cost $38.00 to record, sold 10 million

The Beach Boys

Brian Wilson (1942-), Dennis Wilson (1944-1983), Carl Wilson (1946-1998), Mike Love (1941-), Alan Jardine (1942-) most important of surf groups. Beginning with the cliches of surf they evolved from garage band to art-rock creating a series of recordings that have remained popular and artistic successes. Much admired (and envied) by the Beatles.

I. Recording history during the 1960s: began as family affair (3 brothers, cousin, friend, managed by father).

1. first local release: *Surfin'* 1961 exploited surf themes and terminology, show influences of Four Freshmen, Chuck Berry, and Bill Haley
2. first national release on Capitol: *Surfin' Safari* 1962
    first album: *Surfin' USA* (1963) ignited national surf craze
3. Brian Wilson became band's producer, resulting in more personal, quirkier recordings:
    -   *Surfer Girl* 1963, *California Girls* 1965, *Deuce Coup, I Get Around*
4. ***Pet Sounds*** 1966, BBoys most important recording (said to be a reaction to Beatles' *Rubber Soul*):
    -   one of the first concept albums, unified by themes of isolation and search for emotional security (influenced *Sgt. Pepper's*)
    -   unusual instrumental usage
    -   because of its unconventionality, Pet Sounds was not a popular success in US
5. ***Good Vibrations*** 1966, BBoys best selling single took 6 months to record in 4 different studios at a cost of $30,000
6. *Smile* 1967, controversial album never released as planned
7. left Capitol in 1969

II. Unique musical characteristics:

    1.   complex vocals using
- falsetto counterpoint, non vibrato
- dense jazz-derived harmony (from Four Freshmen)

    2.   unusual choice and use of instruments:
- strings, English horn, bass harmonica, harpsichord (*Pet Sounds*)
- theremin, organ, unusual percussion (*Good Vibrations*)
- prerecorded sound effects (musique concrete) (*Pet Sounds*)

    3.   recording techniques: influenced by Phil Spector:
- Wall of Sound overdubbing

    4.   complex forms - (*Good Vibrations*: A B A B C D E B)

---

*Addenda: Surf Terminology**

Knowledge of surf terminology is essential for a full comprehension of some lyrics. In addition, many of these words, along with those from the Beats and African-American slang have become part of contemporary American speech:

Awesome: great
Bogus: false, unbelievable
Bummer: bad
Dork or Geek: someone who behaves inappropriately
Gnarly: dangerous
Gremlin: a beginning surfer
Hang Five/10: to place five (or 10) toes over the nose of the surfboard
Honeys: female surfers
Kook: an inexperienced surfer
Rad: very good
Shred: to surf aggressively
Stoked: to be happy, excited
Surfaris: a surfing trip
Wipe Out: to fall off a surfboard (also known as "Eating it")
Woodie: a station wagon with wood side paneling

* from "Surfin Dictionary", liner notes to CD "Cowabunga! The Surf Box"

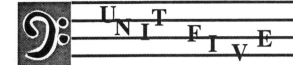

Soul (1960s)

Aretha Franklin. CORBIS-BETTMANN.

A continuation of Rhythm and Blues, Soul, as it became known in the 1960s, completed the process begun in the late 1940s of presenting Black music to mainstream White America. The rise of commercially successful Black music should be seen in the larger context of the achievements of the Civil rights movement of the 1960s (see below). Important styles of soul were developed in Detroit and Memphis at the Mo-Town and Stax studios, in Chicago and Philadelphia. Also during this period James Brown created a more uncompromising music that appealed primarily to Blacks.

Soul to Funk

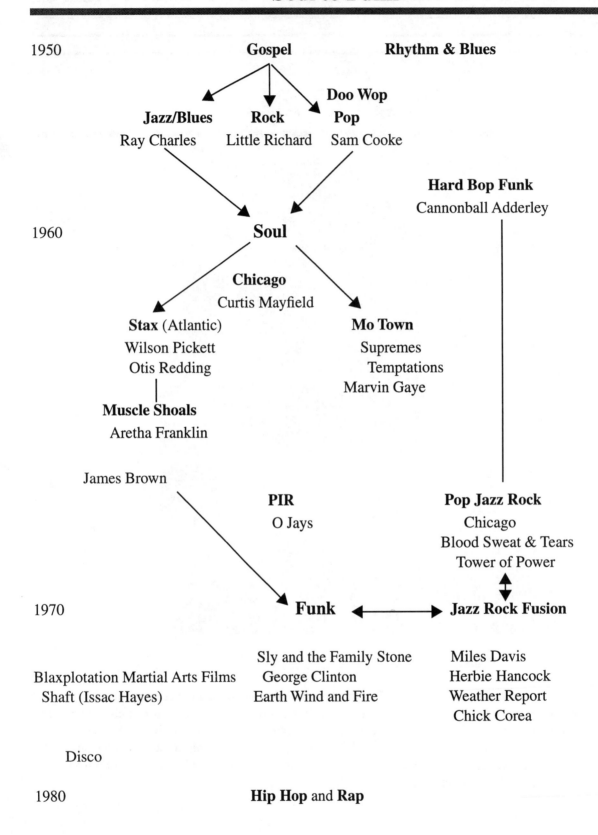

1950   **Gospel**   **Rhythm & Blues**

Doo Wop

Jazz/Blues   **Rock**   **Pop**

Ray Charles   Little Richard   Sam Cooke

Hard Bop Funk

Cannonball Adderley

1960   **Soul**

Chicago

Curtis Mayfield

Stax (Atlantic)   **Mo Town**

Wilson Pickett   Supremes

Otis Redding   Temptations

                        Marvin Gaye

Muscle Shoals

Aretha Franklin

James Brown

                  PIR   **Pop Jazz Rock**

                  O Jays   Chicago

                          Blood Sweat & Tears

                          Tower of Power

1970   **Funk**   **Jazz Rock Fusion**

            Sly and the Family Stone   Miles Davis

Blaxplotation Martial Arts Films   George Clinton   Herbie Hancock

Shaft (Issac Hayes)   Earth Wind and Fire   Weather Report

                                      Chick Corea

      Disco

1980   **Hip Hop** and **Rap**

Some specific characteristics of Soul, especially derived from the Gospel element of R&B include:

1.   church-derived vocal techniques (pioneered in particular by Ray Charles):
    -   call and response
    -   spoken passages
    -   wide vibrato and exuberant delivery
2.   secular lyrics. In male singers often sexual bragging (soul man), macho
3.   unflagging presence of bass and drums

Mo-Town's Golden Years

During the Mid 1960s Mo-town, the first important Black-owned recording company, was a major force in American popular music, with 75% of their carefully controlled products making the national charts. Using mass production techniques analogous to Detroit's automotive assembly line, Mo-Town created a smooth, refined version of soul aimed specifically for adult audiences.

I. Berry Gordy (b. 1929 Detroit) arranger-producer, A&R (artist and repertoire) man, entrepreneur, became America's foremost Black capitalist.

1.   1957 wrote *Reet Petite* for Jackie Wilson
2.   1959 founded Jobete Publishing Co.
3.   1959 borrowed $800 and founded Mo-Town Record Corporation (Hitsville USA)

II. Rise of Mo-Town:

1.   1959 hired William **Smokey Robinson**, as singer, producer
2.   1962 hired Brian Holland, Lamont Dozier, Eddie Holland (**HDH**) production team; will write 28 hits
3.   1964 forms International Talent Management Inc. and hires model Maxine Powell, and dancer Cholly Atkins to train singers
4.   Mo-Town review tours and bookings at prestigious nightclubs
5.   1964-1967 golden age
6.   1971 Gordy moves to Hollywood

III. Musical Characteristics: smooth, refined, sophisticated product aimed at young adults

1.   rich, orchestral bkgs (wall of sound) using strings, saxes and brass
    producer more important than performer
2.   gospel element with tambourine and hand-clapping
3.   latin rhythms including the clave beat
4.   backup band, The Funk Bros adds jazz influence (James Jamerson, electric bass)

IV. Important Groups/Hits (unless otherwise indicated, all performers from Detroit):

1.   The Miracles: *You've Really Got A Hold On Me* 1962, *Mickey's Money*
2.   Mary Wells, began recording at age 17: *My Guy* 1964, *The One Who Really Loves You*
3.   The Marvelettes, Mo-Town's only girl group: *Please Mr. Postman*, 1st #1 hit 1962
4.   **Martha and the Vandellas**, Martha Reeves first worked as secretary in A&R Dept.:
    •   *Heat Wave* 1963,
    •   *Dancing In The Streets* 1964, *Quicksand*
5.   **Marvin Gaye** (1939-1984), first hired as drummer, then singer and arranger
    •   *Pride and Joy* 1963
    •   *How Sweet It Is To Be Loved By You* 1964
    •   *I Heard It Through The Grapevine* 1968

- Left MoTown to produce more controversial songs
  - *What's Goin' On* 1970
- Shot to death by father

6. Jr. Walker and the All Stars, tenor sax R&B, Mo-Town's only instrumental star: *Shotgun* 1965
7. The Four Tops:
    - *I Can't Help Myself* 1965
8. The **Temptations**, Mo-Town's top male group, only group to come up from the South:
    - *The Way You Do The Things You Do* 1964
    - *Ain't Too Proud To Beg*
    - *My Girl* 1965
9. Diana Ross and the **Supremes**, most successful with 12 #1 hits:
    - *Where Did Our Love Go* 1964
    - *Stop, In The Name Of Love* 1965
    - *I Hear A Symphony* 1965

The Supremes © Bettmann/CORBIS

10. Gladys Knight and the Pips: *I Heard It Through The Grapevine* 1968

11.   **Jackson 5**, (with 12 yr old Michael) from Gary: *I Want You Back* 1969

(Stevie Wonder, whose career started out in Mo-Town will be discussed later)

V.   Mo-Town's decline began in 1967 with internal dissension and lack of new talent:

1.   1967 HDH team left
2.   artists like Marvin Gaye and Stevie Wonder chafed under creative restriction and left
3.   eclipsed by Philadelphia soul (Gamble & Huff)

Southern Soul: Atlantic by way of STAX

Atlantic Records, founded in 1947, was another source of soul that tended to retain more Gospel and R&B elements that Mo-Town. Ray Charles and Solomon Burke were already recording soul early in the 1960s when Atlantic began to use several recording studios including STAX in Memphis, and Muscle Shoals, Alabama.

I.   Stax: Founded by Jim **ST**ewart and Estelle **AX**ton in 1958 (original name Satellite) recorded for Atlantic 1960-1968. Important performers included:

1.   house band: **Booker T and the MG's,** (Steve Cropper, guitar, Duck Dunn, bass, Booker T. Jones, keyboard, Al Jackson, drums) integrated ensemble that stressed electric guitar, active bass lines, and parallel horn writing; had their own instrumental hit: *Green Onions* 1962
2.   **Wilson Pickett** (1941-) *In The Midnight Hour* 1965
3.   Sam and Dave: *Soul Man* 1967
4.   **Otis Redding** (1941-1967) influenced by Little Richard and Sam Cooke
     -   specialized in Soul ballads (*Try A Little Tenderness*)
     -   1966 album: *The Otis Redding Dictionary Of Soul*
     -   appeared at Monterey Pop Festival 1967
     -   best selling recording released posthumously *The Dock Of The Bay* 1968
5.   Isaac Hayes: *Theme From Shaft* 1971
6.   Jean Knight: *Mr. Big Stuff* 1970

II.   Muscle Shoals: used all White rhythm section

1.   Percy Sledge: *When A Man Loves A Woman* 1966
2.   Aretha Franklin (b. Memphis 1942-):
     -   began singing in father's church
     -   1960 -1966 mediocre pop recordings with Columbia
     -   soul with Atlantic and at Muscle Shoals and returned to frenzied gospel style of youth: album *I Never Loved A Man The Way I Loved You* (with hit single *Respect* 1967)
     -   *Aretha Live At Fillmore West* (with guest appearance by Ray Charles) 1971
     -   later soul covers of *Eleanor Rigby* and *The Weight* 1969
     -   appeared in The Blues Brothers (1980) singing *Think*

Comparison between Mo-Town and Stax

Mo-Town (Hitsville)	**Stax** (Soulville)
1. Detroit based, Black-owned	Memphis, White-owned (in beginning)
2. all Black performers	integrated performers
3. records aimed at White audience	primarily aimed at Black R&B audience
4. rigid, hierarchical organization assembly line process	loose, accessible to outside input spontaneous
5. producer/composer most important	performers most important
6. smooth, refined controlled pop sound	unemcumbered, raw, closer to R&B
7. Wall of Sound background	clean horns with rhythm section

Other Regional Soul

I. **Chicago:** produced a distinctive soul style in the late 1950s characterized by a smooth, restrained and dignified sound.

    1.   Jerry Butler and **Curtis Mayfield** founded **The Impressions**
       -   *For Your Precious Love* 1958, one of the first soul classics (Veejay)
    2.   later version of group recorded *Gypsy Woman* 1961

II. **Philadelphia:** dominated in the early 60s by American Bandstand Philadelphia began to create a distinctive soul sound in mid 1960s.

    1.   **Kenny Gamble/Leon Huff** created first hit with the Intruders, 1967
       -   formed Philadelphia International Records (**PIR**) 1971, important groups: Harold Melvin and the Blue Notes
          The **O'Jays**: *For The Love Of Money* 1972
    2.   House band: MFSB (Mother, Father, Sister, Brother)
    3.   Clearer sound than Mo-Town created by guitars recording directly into studio board
       -   use of vibes for lighter sound
    4.   PIR paved the way for late 70s Disco

James Brown: Gospel to Soul to Funk to Minimalism

James Brown's music heightened and exaggerated the hysterical side of the secularized chruch experience, creating unique vocal declamations accompanied by dense, complex layers of polyrhythms.

Brown was born 1933 in Georgia and endured difficult childhood of poverty, spending time in reform school before deciding in 1952 to make music his career and forming "The Famous Flames"

I. **Early Gospel and R&B to Soul**

    1.   1956 began recording for King Records (Cincinnati)
       •   *Please, Please, Please,* biggest early hit
       •   *Try Me* 1958, Gospel ballad
       •   *Night Train* 1961, bass begins to be more active
      develops tight touring band ("The hardest working man in show business")

II. **1963 The James Brown Show Live At The Apollo, hit soul album, charted for 66 weeks**

- *I Don't Mind*

III. **Soul To Funk - developed most innovative style**

1. 1964 *Out Of Sight*, pulsating, jerky sax riffs
2. 1965 recorded two most popular tunes
   - *Papa's Got A Brand New Bag*, lean, tight rhythms
   - *I Got You (I Feel Good)* with double time middle section
3. assembles classic band with important sidemen including Maceo Parker, saxophone, and Clyde Stubblefield, drums
   - 1967 *Cold Sweat*, replaces blues chords with vamp
   - 1968 *Say It Loud-I'm Black And I'm Proud*, with Children's Chorus
   - 1969 *Mother Popcorn*, tight horns

IV. **Funk to Minimalism**

forms new band including Bootsie Collins, bass and Catfish Collins, guitar, developing even more rhythmically dominated music

- 1970 *Get (I Feel Like Being A) Sex Machine*, debut of the Collins bros.
- 1972 *Talkin' Loud & Sayin' Nothing*
- 1972 *Get Up (Get Into It And Get Involved)*, minimalism
- 1972 *There It Is*, alternating vamps

V. **Later Recordings**

- 1972 *I Got A Bag Of My Own* studio band including jazzers Michael Brecker and Joe Farrell
- 1973 *Papa Don't Take No Mess Pt. 1*, with Maceo Parker, played in Zaire at "The Rumble In The Jugle"
- *Unity Pt. 1*, Rap with Afrika Bambaataa

Unique Musical Characteristics

emphasizing rhythm over melody with interlocking grid of polyrhythmic strata

1. Vocal: harsh, declamatory (shouting rather than singing), falsetto shrieks coordinated with constant stage movement and dancing (the Mashed Potato and Camel walk)
2. Instrumental: each part maintaining repetitive pattern
   - staccato repeating bass riffs ("the one")
   - choked rhythm guitar
   - horn repeated note punctuations
3. Form: 9th chord vamps replaces blues

James Brown © Neal Preston/CORBIS

Addenda: Important Events in Civil Rights History (1947-1968)

1947: Jackie Robinson joins Brooklyn Dodgers, beginning of the end of the Negro Leagues
1954: Brown vs. Board of Education of Topeka outlaws separate but equal policy
1955: bus boycott in Alabama
1956: Martin Luther King emerges as leader
1957: Federal Troops sent to Little Rock to uphold integration
1960: sit-in at Woolworth in Greensboro, NC
1962: first Blacks admitted to Univ. of Miss.
1963: King's I Have A Dream speech
1964: Congress passes Civil Rights Act
1965: Voting Rights Act
    Selma march
    Malcolm X assassinated
    Watts riots
1967: riots in Detroit, Cleveland, Newark
1968: Martin Luther King assassinated in Memphis

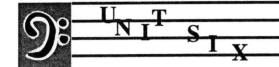

Poetic Interlude
Dylan and the Folk Revival

Bob Dylan, 1969. AMALIE R. ROTHSCHILD/CORBIS-BETTMANN.

Bob Dylan, who brought a new depth of sophistication to rock poetry and later helped collapse the boundaries between rock, folk, and country, became the seminal personality of the 1960s folk revival. He brought to rock from folk a new political awareness, only to reject it in favor of a more personal route, a process copied by the singer-songwriters of the 1970s.

A Dylan 60s Chronology

1941: b. Robert Zimmermann, Hibbing MN, grew up Jewish outcast. Became interested in Rockabilly after hearing Bill Haley and Buddy Holly

1959: Univ. of Minnesota, changed name to Bob Dillon, then Dylan. Taste in music changes to folk after hearing Woody Guthrie

1960: moved to New York's Greenwich Village and visited Guthrie in hospital. Began singing in coffee houses and was discovered by Colombia's John Hammond

1962: 1st album Bob Dylan released to small sales, mostly traditional folk music sung in sarcastic style. Poetry influenced by Jack Kerouac's *Mexico City Blues*

1963: 2nd album *The Free Wheelin' Bob Dylan* included hit *Blowin In The Wind*. Songs exhibiting growing political consciousness. Made important performance at Newport Folk Festival. Began touring with **Joan Baez**

1964: 3rd album *The Times They Are A Changin'*, emerged as major personality in folk music, Next album *Another Side Of Bob Dylan* marked a turning away from politics, first of many-perceived betrayals by folk purists. Became influenced by Beatles

1965: played with new backup band, **The Band**. Released two electric singles, *Subterranean Homesick Blues*, and *Like A Rolling Stone* Performed in new **Folk-Rock** style at Newport Folk Festival. Dylan accused of selling out

released two albums with Paul Butterfield, *Bringing It All Home*, including *Mr. Tambourine Man*, later covered by the Byrds, and *Highway 61 revisited*. Married Sara Lowndes

1966: released double album *Blonde On Blonde*. Broke neck in motorcycle accident, 6 month recuperation at Woodstock. Makes Basement Tapes, released in 1975

1968: *John Wesley Harding* began move away from rock to country

1969: *Nashville Skyline* recorded with country musicians

Some characteristics:

lyrics: influenced by Guthrie (social issues), Beats (cryptic/obscure, susceptible to wide variety of interpretation), Rimbaud and Baudelaire, Brecht, Dylan Thomas and Kafka

music: Charismatic persona more important than pure musical skills: weak deadpan, sarcastic vocal delivery with sardonic humor. Country blues strumming guitar, harmonica

The Folk Song Revival and its Importance to Rock

In championing Civil Rights, and later, the anti-war movement, Folk music brought a political awareness to rock as well as creating more substantive lyrics.

I.   **History:** folk music reemerged with the rise of the new left

1.   Folk music went underground during the politically repressive 1950s
- Sen. Joseph McCarthy communist witch hunts included leftist folk singers
- The Weavers, Woody Guthrie blacklisted
- Seeger subpoenaed by HUAC, cited for contempt and blacklisted until 1967

2.   new commercial form of safe, acceptable folk music appeared in 1958 with **The Kingston Trio's** hit *Tom Dooley*

3.   ABC's TV program Hootenanny

4.   New York's Greenwich Village became center for Folk movement and left wing politics: 1958 folk singers resist city order banning singing in Washington Square. *The Village Voice* founded

5. Sick comics: Mort Sahl, Lennie Bruce, Shelley Berman, Dick Gregory
6. 1960s folk became popular on college campuses along with coffee houses, associated with older beat movement of Kerouac, Ginsberg et al
7. Spirit of political commitment returns as part Kennedy's optimistic New Frontier, rise of student left wing politics:
   - ban the bomb (SANE)
   - peace corps
   - civil rights (CORE)(SNCC)
8. Older singer stage comebacks: Pete Seeger, Odetta

II. **Important groups/performers** of the early 1960s:

1. **Peter Paul and Mary:** their cover of *Blowin In The Wind* helped promote Dylan's career
2. **Joan Baez** (1941-) grew up in Boston of Mexican, Irish descent. Began singing in local coffee houses
   - debuted in front of 13,000 at 1959 Newport Folk Festival, later sellout concert in Carnegie Hall
   - unlike Dylan, remained acoustic folk singer concerned about politics

Simon and Garfunkel © Bettmann/CORBIS

3. **Simon and Garfunkel's** exquisite vocal harmonizations successfully combined literate, intelligent lyrics with a smooth Pop Brill Building musical sensibility to create a gentle and sophisticated body of work fusing folk with pop rock.
   - childhood friends, Paul Simon (1941) and Art Garfunkel (1941) began singing Everly Bros. influenced duos, performing on American Bandstand in 1957.
   - While Garfunkel attended college Simon lived in London before reuniting for six albums.

Simon/Garfunkel Albums

- *Wednesday Morning 3 AM* 1964
  -acoustic version of "Sounds of Silence"
- *Sounds of Silence* 1966
  -overdubbed folk rock version of "Sounds of Silence"
  -acoustic folk "April Come She Will"
- *Parsley Sage Rosemary and Thyme* 1966
  -art rock hints in "Scarborough Canticle"
- *The Graduate* 1968
  - "Mrs. Robinson" (originally Mrs. Roosevelt) charted #1 hit single
- *Bookends* 1968
  - "The Boxer"
  "So Long Frank Lloyd Wright" speaks of the breakup of the duo
- *Bridge Over Troubled Water* 1970
  -gospel Phil Spectoresque hit "Bridge Over Troubled Water"

While Garfunkel pursued a career in films (Catch 22, Carnal Knowledge) Simon continued to explore new musical directions (see Unit XIV).

- 1981 reunion concert in New York's Central Park drew 400,0000.

4. **Phil Ochs** (1940-1976) anti-war singer
5. **Arlo Guthrie**: Woody's son, created cult classic with film "Alice's Restaurant" 1969
6. **Richie Havens** (1941-) created rapid guitar style based on open E tuning

Comparison of Pop Rock with Folk Music

Pop Rock (especially Brill Bldg-Teen Idols)	**Folk**
1. songs deal with love and sex	political concerns, personal freedom
2. marketed for large teen-age audience	small college audience
3. electric, wall of sound	acoustic
4. released in 45 rpm records	33 1/3 albums

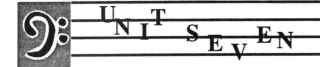

The British Invasion (1964-1967)

The Beatles, 1964. CORBIS-BETTMANN.

In a spiritual decline following the assassination of John F. Kennedy, and cloying with a pop-style of rock that had lost its initial excitement, America was ripe for the cultural invasion of the British, who achieved this rejuvenation, not initially through new, original material, but by recycling older American Blues, R&B, and Rock & Roll classics in a more exuberant, sophisticated albeit raunchier style. The two most important groups emerging during the period were the Beatles and The Rolling Stones.

39

I. Social Conditions in Britain during the 1950s marked by decline and boredom, post-industrial blight.

1. class consciousness more important than in America
2. loss of empire: India (1947), Palestine (1948), Gold Coast (1957), Malaya (1957), Kenya (1961)
3. economic hardship, with wartime rationing until 1954, unemployment
4. important writers reflecting the decline in England's status include:
   - George Orwell: *Nineteen Eighty Four* (1949)
   - William Golding: *The Lord Of The Flies* (1954)
   - Anthony Burgess: *A Clockwork Orange*
   - while England most popular writer retreated into Anglo-saxon mythology:
     - J.R.R.Tolkein: *The Lord Of The Rings* (1955)
5. idle middle class spawned stereotypical gangs, especially:
   - **Teddy Boys** and **Rockers**: leather, motorcycle jacketed greasers, preferred Rockabilly
   - **Mods** (Modernists): fancy dressed amphetamine users

II. Important Urban centers creating distinct styles:

1. **Liverpool**: England's most important port where American recordings readily available
   - **Skiffle**: mixture of Dixieland Jazz and Country Blues
     - Lonnie Donegan *Rock Island Line* 1956
   - The Merseybeat: guitar dominated combos: electric lead guitar, rhythm guitar, electric bass guitar, drums
   - groups included Gerry And The Pacemakers, The Searchers
2. **Manchester**, industrial neighbor of Liverpool: two popular groups: The Hollies (named after Buddy Holly) formed by Graham Nash in 1962, Herman's Hermits, targeted very young audience
3. **London**: England's cultural center and home of recording industry
   - pop rock scene dominated by Dave Clark 5, and Petulia Clark
   - influenced by blues, especially Chicago blues (Muddy Waters)
   - Alexis Korner (1928-) entrepreneur, fostered blues scene with string of night clubs
   - many musicians came from a background of avant garde art

The Beatles (1960-1969)

Without serious competition as the most important group in rock history, the Beatles were both conservative (using proven, African-American derived models) and innovative (especially in their collaborations with 5th Beatle George Martin). They rearticulated rock's previous styles in careful yet exuberant covers, then constantly experimenting, pioneered in new directions of Art Rock, whose implications were to rebound through the next two decades. So comprehensive was their stylistic range that it is meaningless to list style characteristics, as these changed drastically from year to year. Somehow they managed to create a repertoire that appealed both to the teen and the sophisticated listener. Like Elvis, their only serious competitor, they became larger-than-life world figures and their opinions helped shape the hippie generation of the 1960s. Unlike many rock bands, the Beatles were a true group in which synergy played an important role, as testified by the comparable lack of success in the subsequent solo albums.

Lennon & McCartney: The Fab Two

While the contributions of George Harrison and Ringo Starr to the success of the Beatles were important, it is the repertoire of songs written in synergistic collaboration by Lennon and McCartney that form the central body of work that has given the Beatles its unique place in music. At first working closely together, they began evolving their own distinctive voices, arriving at different styles by the time of the breakup of the group in 1969. The following is a comparison of some of the differences that evolved between the two:

	Lennon	McCartney
General:	dark, pessimistic	light, optimistic
	extreme	moderate
	art	Pop
	avant garde	mainstream
Lyrics:	words written first	lyrics less important
	autobiographical, confessional	3rd person narratives
	philosophical, emotional states	stories, portraits
	acerbic, obtuse	sentimental, charming, comfortable
Music:	rhythmic emphasis	melodic/harmonic (Music Hall)
	angular	smooth
	lean, stark	rich, opulent

The following is a chronological list of selected songs showing the principal creators. Generally the primary composer sang the lead melody. Songs in the middle of the chart are more representative of true collaborations:

Lennon	McCartney
Hard Day's Night	And I Love Her
If I Fell (*Hard Day's Night 1964*)	
I'm a Loser	I'll Follow the Sun (*Beatles for Sale 1964*)
You've Got to Hide Your Love Away	Yesterday (*Help 1965*)
We Can Work It Out (*single 1965*)	
Tomorrow Never Knows	Here There and Everywhere (*Revolver 1966*)
Strawberry Fields Forever	Penny Lane (*single 1997*)
A Day in the Life (*Sgt. Pepper's Lonely Hearts Club 1967*)	
Happiness Is a Warm Gun	Blackbird (*The Beatles 1968*)
Ballad of John and Yoko (single 1969)	Hey Jude (*single 1968*)
Mean Mr. Mustard/Polythene Pam	She Came in through the Bathroom Window (*Abbey Road 1969*)
Solo albums begin	
Mother	Junk
Well Well Well	Teddy
Working Class Hero (*Plastic Ono Band 1970*)	Maybe I'm Amazed (*McCartney 1970*)

Beatles History

I. Beginnings

1. 1940-43: **John Lennon, Ringo Starr** (Richard Starkey), **Paul McCartney, George Harrison**, born in Liverpool to middle-class working families
2. 1956-58: John and Paul met and played in The Quarrymen. George joined in 1958
3. name changed to "Johnny And The Moondogs", to "Silver Beatles", to **Beatles**

II. Early Career

1. 1959-1960: Stu Sutcliffe, art student joined group on bass. Pete Best added on drums. First gigs in Hamburg
2. **Brian Epstein** became manager. Sutcliffe quit (later dies of brain tumor) Paul plays bass. Continuous gigs in Hamburg and at the Cavern in Liverpool. First recording in Hamburg, *My Bonnie* backing up Phil Sheridan
3. Beatles cover American artists: Berry, Holly, Little Richard, Mo-Town, etc.

III. Beatlemania

1. 1962: signs contract with EMI, **George Martin** (1929-) becomes producer. Ringo Starr replaces Best. *Love Me Do*, written by John and Paul in 1957 reached #21 on the charts. Beatles voted best Liverpool band
2. 1963: *I Want To Hold Your Hand* first hit in U.S. *Please, Please, Me* first album, held #1 position for 30 weeks
3. 1964: 1st U.S. tour. Ed Sullivan Show broke viewer record. Richard Lester's *Hard Days' Night* released to popular and critical acclaim

IV. Mature Albums

1. **Rubber Soul** introduced sitar. *Help* 2nd Lester film. Shea Stadium concert and Jesus controversy
2. 1966: last concert appearance in San Francisco. **Revolver** introduced psychedelic effects, tape manipulation. John met Yoko Ono. Interest in Eastern religion
3. 1967: two important singles *Strawberry Fields Forever, Penny Lane. Sgt. Pepper's Lonely Hearts Club Band* concept album (said to be influenced by Beach Boys' *Pet Sounds*) used tape manipulation, symphony orchestra, Indian instruments, segues and cyclical form

V. Decline and breakup

1. 1967: Brian Epstein died of pill overdose, Beatles studied TM with Maharishi Mahesh Yogi
2. Film *Magical Mystery Tour* fails
3. 1968: Apple Corps formed. *The Beatles* (The White Album), mostly simple solo songs, released
4. 1969: *Abbey Road* last great album recorded with Martin. John and Yoko marry
5. 1970: Beatles dissolved
6. 1980: John Lennon murdered in New York

VI. Early Solo Albums

McCartney:	Lennon:	Harrison:	Starr:
McCartney	*Plastic Ono Band*	*All Things Must Pass*	*Sentimental Journey*
Ram		*Concert for Bangladesh*	*Beaucoup of Blues*
(pop rock)	(primal scream)	(feel good karma)	(standards)

The Released Albums and Important Singles of the Beatles (British Releases)

1963

Please Please Me, released March 22, **side one**: I Saw Her Standing There; Anna; Chains; Boys; Ask Me Why; Please Please Me. **side two**: Love Me Do; P.S. I Love You; Baby Its You; Do You Want To Know A Secret; A Taste Of Honey; There's A Place; Twist And Shout

With The Beatles, released November 22, **side one**: It Won't Be Long Now; All I've Got To Do; All My Loving; Don't Bother Me; Little Child; 'Till There Was You; Please Mister Postman. **side two**: Roll Over Beethoven; Hold Me Tight; You Really Got A Hold On Me; I Wanna Be Your Man; Devil In Her Heart; Not A Second Time; Money

I Want To Hold Your Hand/This Boy released November 29

1964

A Hard Days' Night; released July 10, **side one**: A Hard Day's Night; I Should Have Known Better; If I Fell; I'm Just Happy To Dance With You; And I Love Her; Tell Me Why; Can't Buy Me Love. **side two**: Any Time At All; I'll Cry Instead; Things We Said Today; When I Get Home; You Can't Do That; I'll Be Back

Beatles For Sale, released December 1964, **side one**: No Reply; I'm A Loser; Baby's In Black; Rock And Roll Music; I'll Follow the Sun; Mr. Moonlight; Kansas City. **side two**: Eight Days A Week; Words Of Love; Honey Don't; Every Little Thing; I Don't Want To Spoil The Party; What You're Doing; Everybody's Trying To Be My Baby

1965

Help! released August 6, **side one**: Help!; The Night Before; You've Got To Hide Your Love Away; I Need You; Another Girl; You're Going To Lose That Girl; Ticket To Ride. **side two**: Act Naturally; It's Only Love; You Like Me Too Much; Tell Me What You See; I've Just Seen A Face; Yesterday; Dizzy Miss Lizzy

We Can Work It Out/Day Tripper, released December 3

Rubber Soul, released December 3, **side one**: Drive My Car; Norwegian Wood; You Won't See Me; Nowhere Man; Think For Yourself; The Word; Michelle. **side two**: What Goes On; Girl; I'm Looking Through You; In My Life; Wait; If I Needed Someone; Run For Your Life

1966

Revolver, released August 5, **side one**: Taxman; Eleanor Rigby; I'm Only Sleeping; Love You To; Here There And Everywhere; Yellow Submarine; She Said She Said. **side two**: Good Day Sunshine; And Your Bird Can Sing; For No One; Doctor Roberts; I Want To Tell You; Got To Get You Into My Life; Tomorrow Never Knows

1967

Strawberry Fields Forever/Penny Lane, released February 17

Sgt. Pepper's Lonely Hearts Club Band, released June 1, **side one**: Sgt. Pepper's Lonely Hearts Club Band; With A Little Help From My Friends; Lucy In The Sky With Diamonds; Getting Better; Fixing A Hole; She's Leaving Home; Being For The Benefit Of Mr. Kite. **side two**: Within You Without You; When I'm Sixty-Four; Lovely Rita; Good Morning Good Morning; Sgt. Pepper's Lonely Hearts Club Band (Reprise) A Day In The Life

All You Need Is Love/Baby Your A Rich Man, released July 7

Hello Goodby/I Am The Walrus, released November 24

Magical Mystery Tour, Extended Play, released December 8, **side one**: Magical Mystery Tour, Your Mother Should Know. **side two**: I Am The Walrus. **side three**: The Fool On The Hill; Flying. **side four**: Blue Jay Way

1968

Lady Madonna/The Inner Light, released March 15

Hey Jude/Revolution, released August 30

The Beatles (aka *The White Album*), released November 22, **side one**: Back In The USSR; Dear Prudence; Glass Onion; Oh-La-Di-Ob-La-Da; Wild Honey Pie; The Continuing Story Of Bungalow Bill; While My Guitar Gently Weeps, Happiness Is A Warm Gun. **side two**: Martha My Dear; I'm So Tired; Blackbird; Piggies; Rocky The Raccoon; Don't Pass Me By; Why Don't We Do It In The Road; I Will; Julia. **side three**: Birthday; Yer Blues; Mother Nature's Son; Everybody's Got Something To Hide Except Me And My Monkey; Sexy Sadie; Helter Skelter; Long, Long, Long. **side four**: Revolution I; Honey Pie; Savoy Truffle; Cry Baby Cry; Revolution 9; Goodnight

1969

Yellow Submarine, released January 17, **side one**: Yellow Submarine, Only A Northern Song; All Together Now, Hey Bulldog, It's All Too Much; All You Need Is Love. **side two**: soundtrack to movie by George Martin

Get Back/Don't Let Me Down, released April 11

The Ballad Of John And Yoko/Old Brown Shoe, released May 30

Abbey Road, released September 26, **side one**: Come Together; Something; Maxwell's Silver Hammer; Oh! Darling; Octopus's Garden; I Want You. **side two**: Here Comes The Sun; Because; You Never Give Me Your Money; Sun King; Mean Mr. Mustard; Polythene Pam; She Came In Through The Bathroom Window; Golden Slumbers; Carry That Weight; The End; Her Majesty

1970

Let It Be, released May 8, **side one**: Two Of Us; Dig A Pony; Across The Universe; I Me Mine; Dig It; Let It Be; Maggie Mae. **side two**: I've Got A Feeling; The One After 909; The Long And Winding Road; For You Blue; Get Back

The Rolling Stones

The Rolling Stones, London's most important blues-derived band and only serious rival to the Beatles, consciously portrayed a mean, working class persona, largely manufactured by their manager, Andrew Loog Oldham. This distinction, from the sweet chic image of the Beatles, was also reflected musically, by emphasizing a cruder, elemental type of Rock & Roll. As the decade of the 60s wore on, the Stones were cast in the more typical counterculture role associated with rock, while the Beatles became associated with art, and older, more sophisticated listeners.

The Rolling Stones © Hulton-Deutsch Collection/CORBIS

The 60s Stones

I. **Formation** 1963:

1. **Keith Richards**, lead guitar; **Mick Jagger**, vocals, harmonica; **Brian Jones**, rhythm guitar, additional instruments; Dick Taylor, bass; Tony Chapman, drums; later **Bill Wyman** replaces Taylor, **Charlie Watts**, replaces Chapman, Ron Wood and Mick Taylor replace D. Taylor and Jones.
2. most had upper middle class bkgs, some were art students
3. manager Andrew Loog Oldham created image of lower class vulgarity, misogyny, suggested they wear dirty, unmatching clothes, helped Jagger develop narcissistic, exhibitionist stage demeanor
4. first recordings mostly Chicago blues and Buddy Holly covers:
    *   *Come On* (Chuck Berry)
    *   *I Want to be Loved* (Willie Dixon) 1963
    *   *Not Fade Away* sold 100,000 1964

- *I Just Want to Make Love to You* (Muddy Waters) 1964
5. first album 1964: *The Rolling stones*

II. **Popularity** achieved 1964 during second U.S. tour

1. began writing original material (Jagger-words, Richards-music)
2. 1965 *(I Can't Get No) Satisfaction* reaches #1 on American charts

Important Albums and American Singles

	1965	
The Rolling Stones, Now!		*Satisfaction*
Out Of Our Heads		*Get Off My Cloud*
	1966	
Big Hits (High Tide and Green Grass)		*19th Nervous Breakdown*
Aftermath		*Paint it Black*
	1967	
Beneath The Buttons		*Ruby Tuesday*
Their Satanic Majesties Request		*Lets Spend The Night Together*
	1968	
Beggars Banquet		*Jumpin' Jack Flash*
Street Fighting Man		
	1969	
Let It Bleed		*Honky Tonk Woman*
	1971	
Sticky Fingers		*Brown Sugar*
Wild Horses		
	1972	
Exile On Main Street		
	1973	
		You Can't Always Get What You Want
		Angie

III. Setbacks:

1. Brian Jones found dead in swimming pool July 1969
2. **Altamount**: December 1969 free concert by Stones in San Francisco draws 300,000. Members of the Hells Angels, hired as security force kills 18-year-old Berkeley student, spelled end of hippie era of peace and love, recorded in movie **Gimme Shelter**

Other British Groups

After the early success of the Beatles and The Rolling Stones, a second wave of equally popular groups followed.

I.   The Who

Combing an odd mix of garage-band high volume primitivism with art rock, the Who filled a niche between the Beatles and the Stones. Unlike the Stones and the Kinks, the Who were less influenced by Blues.

1962   **Roger Daltry** (1944-) a sheet metal worker forms the Detours and hires **John Entwistle** (1944-) on bass, talks Daltry into hiring **Pete Townshend** (1945-) on guitar.

1963   **Keith Moon** (1947-1978) hired on drums. Develops into one of Rock's most flamboyant performers. Increases size of drum set. Townshend's (a student in Art school) intellectual interests immediately clash with Daltry's lower class sensibilities resulting in numerous clashes.

1964   During gig Pete accidentally smashed his guitar, crowd reacts in hysterics. Moon responds by trashing his drums. Auto stage destruction becomes a standard feature of Who. Pete Meadon becomes manager and molds them into a Mod persona, called "High Numbers", later The Who.

Who begin association with Jim Marshall. Begins stacking Marshall Amps for increased volume and distortion effects.

1965   "I Can't Explain" Beatles-style pop song becomes first hit
   -       sold 104,000 copies. "Anyway, Anyhow, Anywhere" attempted to create less pop sound, uses distortion and feedback.

Townshend begins writing original material. Leadership shifts from Daltry to Townshend.

   "My Generation" reaches #2 in UK. Stuttering lyric used to suggest amphetamine high. Who's first LP *My Generation* released. "The Ox" Moon feature

1966   2nd LP *A Quick One, Happy Jack* lightweight pop reaches #3 in UK *"Boris The Spider"* features Entwistle as composer/bassist

1967   Monterey Pop appearance brings first important US exposure **"I Can See For Miles"** use of Dissonance /*"Armenia"* use of guitar effects. "Magic Bus" Bo Diddley influenced

1968   Townshend becomes attracted to Indian guru, Meher Baba. Gives up drugs but careful not to publicize fact for fear of alienating hippies.
   3rd LP *The Who Sell Out*

1969   Rock opera **"Tommy"** included "Pinball Wizard" which reaches #4 in UK. Rock's first and most successful opera. 4th LP *Tommy*, released

1971   5th album *Who's Next*. Only LP to reach #1 in UK *Baba O'Reilly*-electronic effects
   Moon's health and playing deteriorate

1972   Moon appears as nun in Zappa's film "200 Motels"

1973   *Quadrophenia* recorded

1978   *"Who Are You"* based on Sufi chants. Moon dies from accidental overdose of pills

   importance:
       -helped establish "Power Trio" (lead guitar, bass guitar, drums)
       -created Rock Opera
       -popularized stage destruction

II. Eric Burdon (1941-) and **The Animals**: covered R&B and folk songs, especially *House Of The Rising Sun* 1964.

III. **The Yardbirds** featured three great electric guitarists:

  1. **Eric Clapton** (1945-), blues-oriented player, left to form **Cream**
  2. **Jeff Beck** (1944-), used feedback and other psychedelic effects, formed new group with Rod Stewart (1945-) in 1967
  3. **Jimmy Page** (1944-), experimented with bowing the guitar, eventually formed **Led Zeppelin** for a time Beck and Page played together in a power quartet

ERIC CLAPTON: *early career*

One of Rock's most purist Blues oriented performer, Clapton's early career with many changes in sidemen, can be divided into two phases:

-   early exploration of guitar virtuosity (1960's)
-   pop success featuring vocals with country flavored originals ("Lay Down Sally") and covers (1970's)

Born Eric Clapp 1945

-   attended Art school
-   influenced by Blues men, especially Robert Johnson, Muddy Waters, John Lee Hooker and Elmore James

Clapton's Changing Bands

I. Yardbirds 1963

"Baby What's Wrong" -clean, single-line solo
left after disagreement over pop direction
given nickname "Slowhand"

II. John Mayall's Bluesbreakers (1965)

Keyboardist Mayall,12 yrs older than Clapton, was London's father of Blues. Also influenced Mick Taylor, Jack Bruce and Mick Fleetwood "Ramblin' On MY Mind", Clapton's first vocal, tribute of Robert Johnson "Hideaway" wailing treble solo

"Clapton Is God" graffiti appears in London

III. Cream 1966 (with Jack Bruce, bass, Ginger Baker, drums) first important power trio, heavy emphasis on Jazz-like improv.

"Crossroads" Robert Johnson cover
"Sunshine of your Life" dominated by bass riff

IV. Blind Faith 1969 (with keyboard-vocalists Steve Winwood)
"supergroup" more commercial than Cream
"Presence of the Lord" early Clapton commercial original

V. Delaney and Bonnie 1969 shows Clapton's growing interest in Country Rock
"Comin' Home" Clapton original influenced by the Band's "Big Pink"

VI. Clapton's first Solo Album 1970

"After Midnight" J.J. Cales gospel-soul influenced tune with STAX-like horns

VII. Derek and the Dominos 1970 collaboration at times with Duane Allman recorded some of Clapton's most commercially successful tunes, including "Layla" (based on Clapton's love for George Harrison's wife) "Evil" Willie Dixon cover

Later Clapton hits:

covers: "I Shot The Sheriff" (Marley 1974, "Knockin On Heaven's Door (Dylan) 1975 "Cocaine" (J.J. Cale) 1977
country style original "Lay Down Sally" 1977

IV. The Kinks: Ray Davies, Dave Davies, Peter Quaife, Mick Avory: proto-punk blend of blues and distortion, the Kinks assumed an ever more blatantly anti-establishment posture than the Stones.

- *You Really Got Me* 1964

Art Rock (Progressive Rock)

Inspired by the 1967 Beatles concept album, *Sgt. Peppers Lonely Hearts Club Band*, many English groups experimented with combining elements of rock, classical, and avant garde music. The creators of art rock usually worked with collaborators, for relatively few musicians had equal expertise in both rock and classical. Some aspects of art rock will influence glam/glitter of the 1970s.

I. Characteristics:

1. diversification of instrumental timbre: ranged from simple addition of one or two non-rock instruments (such as cello, flute, French horn etc.) to combining full symphony orchestra with rock group
2. electronic instruments (synthesizers), tape effects ("musique concrete")
3. world music influence, especially India, Africa
4. lengthening duration of individual song past the typical 3:00 time span of pop songs
   - popularity of double albums (all helped through establishment of FM radio)
5. full length planning of album throughout to create overall theme through use of:
   - music conceived as multi-movement works akin to symphonies:
     - segues (linking up of songs without pauses)
     - return of earlier material (cyclical form)
   - cover artwork important
6. use of scales (or modes) not usually found in rock
7. time signatures other than 4/4 or 3/4
8. minimalist repeating rhythms

Art Rock aimed for a sophisticated, older audience of listeners in their 20s

II. Pink Floyd (named after two American bluesmen **Pink** Anderson and **Floyd** Council) Syd Barrett, Roger Waters, Richard Wright, and David Gilmour created most influential of British Art Rock.

1.   two landmark recordings:
     - *Dark Side Of The Moon* 1973 (recorded at Abbey Road) one of rock's best selling albums
     - *The Wall* 1979 allegorical video
   - used extensive synthesizer and musique concrete (opening heartbeat)
   - segued concept album (Wizard of Oz?)
   - minimalism and asymmetric time signatures (7/4)
   - laser light shows

III. Other Important groups and works:

1.   **The Moody Blues**: *Nights In White Satin* 1967; *Days Of Future Passed* 1968 popularized keyboard synthesizer mellotron
2.   **Emerson, Lake and Palmer**, classically trained players
3.   **King Crimson**: formed by Robert Fripp in 1969
4.   **Jethro Tull**: flutist Ian Anderson combined jazz with J.S.Bach
5.   **Electric Light Orchestra**: developed elaborate stage show with lasers
6.   **Yes**: long lasting group founded in 1968

two German synthesizer bands:

7.   **Kraftwerk** (Florien Schneider and Ralf Hutter): synthesizer duo that influenced disco and rap
8.   **Tangerine Dream**

(**Frank Zappa**, the most important American composer of Art Rock, will be discussed later.)

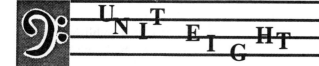

Back in the U.S.A.-Acid Rock (1965-1970)

Janis Joplin, 1969. CORBIS-BETTMANN.

The Legacy of the Beats

Much of the motivation behind the social upheaval of the mid 1960s hippie revolution was the simplified and partially understood legacy of a loosely knit group of writers and intellectuals collectively known as the Beat Generation. Beginning in New York after WWII, its center of gravity shifted in the early 1950s to San Francisco.

I. Important writers:

1. **William S. Burroughs** (1914-) father figure of the beats. *Junkie* 1953, first published novel *Naked Lunch*, most influential and controversial novel (1959). Later collaborated with U2, Tom Waits and Kurt Cobain. Influenced Punk.
2. **Jack Kerouac** (1922-1969) *On The Road* (written in 1951, published in 1957) gave the beat movement national attention. Important jazz-influenced poems: **Mexico City Blues** 1955
3. **Allen Ginsberg** (1927-1997): most prominent poet and social activist: *Howl* 1956. Central figure in the Hippie era

Opening of *Howl*

> I saw the best minds of my generation
> destroyed by madness, starving
> hysterical naked
> dragging themselves thru the negro streets
> at dawn looking for an angry
>   fix,
> angelheaded hipsters burning for the
> ancient heavenly connection to the
>   starry dynamo in the machinery of the night.

4. Gary Snyder (1930-) explored Zen Buddhism
5. Lawrence Ferlinghetti (1919-) founded City Lights Bookstore in San Francisco, 1953

II. Beat philosophy: define one's own morality

1. search for personal freedom and life style, existentialism spontaneity and the communication of deep feelings
2. rejection of American materialistic, capitalistic society and bourgeois morality
3. drug use (alcohol, marijuana and amphetamines) homosexuality
4. embracement of elements of eastern religion (esp. Zen)
5. identification with lower class (glorification of hobo)
6. identification with African-American culture, especially jazz (Norman Mailer: *"The White Negro"* 1958)

The Hippie Movement

Unlike the beat movement, which remained a small, elitist group, the subsequent hippie counterculture directly affected millions. Because of its liberal climate, connection with the Beats, and proximity of several colleges, San Francisco became the epicenter from which the movement spread across the country. Accompanying this social revolution was a new form of rock, Acid (or psychedelic) rock.

I. Important events in development of Hippie scene:

1. Sept. 1965: term Hippies coined by *San Francisco Examiner* writer Michael Fallon
2. Oct. 1965 Allen Ginsberg leads first hippie gathering at Longshoremen's Hall
3. Jan. 1966: Ken Kesey's Merry Pranksters host Trips Festival which attracted 6600. Appearing with Kesey is Neal Cassidy (hero of *On The Road*)
4. 1966: Diggers, former members of San Francisco Mime Troupes, begin giving away free food
5. Aug. 1966: Beatles perform last tour

6. Oct. 1966: LSD (discovered in 1943) becomes illegal substance
7. Jan. 1967: 20,000 people attend First Human Be-In held at Golden Gate State Park
8. Bill Graham opens Fillmore West
9. 1967: "summer of love," 50,000 hippies residing in Haight-Ashberry
10. 1967: Monterey Pop, features Janis Joplin, Otis Redding, The Who, Jimi Hendrix, et al
11. Dec, 1969: Altamount

II. **Hippie philosophy and life-style:** essentially a hedonistic "do your own thing" philosophy that represented a reaction to the perceived repressive conservative mores of the 1950s. Typical hippie profile: white middle-class college educated, between 16-30 yrs old.

1. dissatisfaction with establishment created passive drop-out mentality
2. egalitarian communalism and tribalism
3. free love (by 1966 more than 6 million women using birth control pill)
4. drug use for enhanced creativity and quasi-religious experience
   - LSD (lysergic acid diethylamide), especially Owsley acid (Augustus Owsley Stanley)
   - Timothy Leary, guru of LSD (turn on, tune in, drop out)
   - mescaline (from peyote)
5. interest in eastern religions, including Hare Krishna, Transcendental Meditation, astrology
   - religious texts: Tibetan Book Of The Dead, I Ching, Gurdjieff-Ouspensky
6. initially, apolitical pacifist, later, involvement in anti-war movement

III. **Literature**

1. influential books:
   - Ken Kesey: *One Flew Over The Cuckoo's Nest*
   - Hermann Hesse: *Steppenwolf, Journey To The East* et al
   - Robert Heinlein: *Stranger In A Strange Land*
   - Carlos Castaneda: *The Teaching of Don Juan, A Yaqui Way Of Knowledge* et al
2. the development of the underground press, by 1969 over 500 underground newspapers reached a readership of one million
   - L.A. Free Press 1964
   - San Francisco Oracle 1966
   - Underground Press Syndicate formed in 1967
3. the New Journalism reflected underground style:
   - *Rolling Stone* founded in San Francisco in 1967
   - Tom Wolfe: *The Electric Acid Kool Aid Test*
   - Hunter S. Thompson: *Fear And Loathing In Las Vegas*
   - Norman Mailer: *Armies Of The Night*

Acid Rock

Acid (or psychedelic) rock, a term coined to identify the music of the hippie revolution, was not a unified musical style but rather reflected a similar life style. Many players began in Dylanesque folk or country traditions before going amplified.

I. **Acid Rock:** some generalizations:

1. garage band mentality: deliberate amateurishness, rejection of slick professionalism, free concerts, encouragement of bootleg tapes
2. extended instrumental improvisations
3. use of sitar and the drone for hypnotic effect

4. guitar sound effects: feedback
5. emphasis on visuals:
    - liquid light shows
    - psychedelic poster art: large distorted balloon letters against bright, solid color background

II. Important San Francisco bands: by 1967 over 1000 bands were active in the Bay area, including:

1. **Jefferson Airplane:** formed in 1965 by Marty Balin and Paul Kantner, Grace Slick added in 1966 became the first San Fran. band to sign with major label (RCA). Most commercially successful of Acid bands:
    - albums 1965-1969:
        • *Jefferson Airplane Takes Off* 1966
        • *Surrealistic Pillow* 1967 with hit singles *Somebody to Love* and *White Rabbit*
        • *After Bathing At Baxters* 1967
        • *Crown Of Creation* 1968
        • *Bless Its Pointed Little Head*
        • *Volunteers*
    - band broke up in 1970
2. **The Grateful Dead** (said to be an ancient Egyptian prayer): originally founded by **Jerry Garcia** (1943 -1995) and Bob Weir as "The Warlocks", other members include Phil Lesch, bass, Ron "Pig-pen" McKernan (1945-1973), and drummers Mickey Hart and Bill Kreutzmann along with several keyboard players
    - their diverse musical background insured an eclectic, quirky mix of styles:
        • Garcia: folk/country
        • Pig Pen: blues
        • Lesch: avant garde electronics
        • Hart: world music percussion
    - became house band for Ken Kesey's "acid tests" 1965 and added psychedelic improvisations (and changed name to The Grateful Dead)
    - signed contract with Warner Bros.: some important albums:
        • *Grateful Dead* 1967
        • *Anthem Of The Sun* 1968 unified concept album
        • *Aoxomoxoa* 1970 complex album, took 8 months to assemble in studio
    - because albums never achieved commercial success the Dead focused on touring (e.g. 152 shows in 1969) and began developing a unique following known as **"Deadheads"**, which eventually grew to c.100,000
    - *Live/Dead* 1970 double album marked by long improvisations
    - *Workingman's Dead* 1970 and *American Beauty* 1970 focused on simpler, country-flavored narratives like *Truckin'* ("What a long...... strange trip it's been")
    - *Europe*, 1972 Pig-pen's last album
    - era of stadium tours begins in 1974 necessitating giant "Wall of Sound" amplification system consisting of 641 speakers the size of three-story building
    - death of Garcia, 1995
3. **Santana:** formed by Mexican-born guitarist Carlos Santana in 1967
    - Latin flavored tunes featured fiery Santana jazz-tinged solos and the Hammond organ of Gregg Collie backed up by multiple percussion. *Evil Ways*
4. **Other San Francisco Bands**
    - Quicksilver Messenger Service: often compared to Grateful Dead
    - Country Joe And The Fish
    - Steve Miller Band (with Boz Scaggs)

-    Moby Grape

Los Angeles

Featured a harsher, more desperate edge than San Francisco.

III. The Doors: Jim Morrison, poet-singer (1943-1971), Ray Manzarek, keyboard, Robbie Krieger, guitar, John Densmore, drums, became the most popular of the counter-culture bands. Led by the driven personality of Morrison, Doors performances included theatrical elements influenced by Artois and theater of the absurd.

1. Morrison, son of Rear-Admiral, was student of Theater Arts at UCLA when he and Manzarek formed band The Doors after *The Doors of Perception* by Aldous Huxley. Becomes heavy user of LSD. Morrison's poetry influenced by Beats and French Symbolists Beaudelaire, Verlaine, Rimbaud, Brecht (*Alabama Song*)
2. 1967 plays Whisky A Go Go and reached height of popularity:
   - *Break On Through*, first hit single
   - first album: *The Doors*, included hit single *Light My Fire*, and *The End*
3. Morrison adopts Lizard King persona. Controversial Ed Sullivan Show
   Middle albums
   - *Strange Days* 1967
   - *Waiting For The Sun* 1968
   - *The Soft Parade* 1969
   - *Morrison Hotel* 1970
4. growing erratic behavior of Morrison: Miami 1969: arrested for lewd behavior
   - *L.A.Women* 1971 last album include *Riders From The Sky*
5. 1971: Morrison dies of heart attack in Paris
   - *An American Prayer* 1979 includes Morrison poetry

Janis Joplin and Jimi Hendrix

Two important performers who were influenced by both blues and Acid Rock, Janis Joplin and Jimi Hendrix developed unique musical styles as well as became popular exponents of the hippie lifestyle. Both had short, meteoric careers cut short by drug abuse.

I.   Janis Joplin, singer (1943-1970) exemplified the hippie free-spirited individual, and with her exuberant, virtuosic fusion of blues and country became the first female superstar of Rock. Her self-destructive personality led Time Magazine to call her "The Judy Garland of Rock".

1. b. Port Arthur, TX. began singing in coffee houses in Austin. Two important and diverse influences were Bessie Smith and Willie Mae Thornton
2. 1963 hitchhiked to San Francisco, first extant recording *Trouble On My Mind*, with Jorma Kaukonen
3. 1966 Joins Big Brother and The Holding Company
   - first album *Down On Me*
   - electrifies audience at Monterey Pop Festival with *Ball And Chain*
   - 1968 releases *Cheap Thrills* on Columbia, includes *Piece of My Heart*
4. forms Kozmic Blues Band featuring horn section
   - 1969 Album *I Got Dem Ol' Kozmic Blues Again Mama*, includes *Try Just a Little Harder*

5. forms Full Tilt Boogie Band 1970
   - *Pearl*, released 1971 includes *Get It While You Can, Mercedes Benz,* and *Me And Bobby McGee*
6. dies in L.A. on October 4, 1970, of heroin overdose

Jimi Hendrix © Hulton-Deutsch Collection/CORBIS

II. **Jimi Hendrix**, guitarist (Jimmy Hendrix 1942-1970) one of the true geniuses of rock, Hendrix was without peer as a guitarist and helped make the instrument the dominant sound of rock. While associated with the psychedelic movement, Hendrix's roots were in blues.

1. raised in Seattle, listening to Howlin' Wolf, Muddy Waters, and Elmore James
2. enlisted in army parachute corps 1959, released 1961 after accident
3. 1963: played "Chitlin Circuit" with Little Richard, King Curtis, Wilson Pickett
4. 1964: moved to New York with Isely Bros. Inspired by Dylan began to sing and formed band: Jimmy James and the Blue Flames
5. moved to London and formed Jimi Hendrix Experience with Noel Redding, bass, and Mitch Mitchell, drums.
   - record two hit singles: *Hey Joe* and *Purple Haze*
   - sensational debut at Monterey Pop 1967, set guitar on fire
   - albums with The Experience
     • *Are You Experienced?* 1967
     • *Axis: Bold As Love* 1968
     • *Electric Ladyland* 1968
6. 1968: dissolved Experience, builds Electric Ladyland Studio in NY

7. formed "Band of Gypsies" with Buddy Miles, drums, Billy Cox, bass
    Band of Gypsies 1970
8. 1969: Woodstock performance of *Voodoo Chile, Star Spangled Banner*
9. died of overdose of barbiturates, London, 1970

Unique playing characteristics:

1. left-handed, played upside-down guitar
2. awesome technical mastery (the John Coltrane of guitar)
3. master at musical use of effects:
    -   fuzz tone, feedback and distortion, wa wa pedal
4. deafening, high volume important component of style, created power trio and anticipated heavy metal
5. complex harmony influenced by jazz

Frank Zappa

Frank Zappa, composer and social critic (1940-1994) was a unique figure in rock. Combining elements of rock, jazz, psychedelia and classical, Zappa, with his superior musical curiosity and background created an art-rock legacy of more importance and intellectual substance than any of his British counterparts.

I. Background

1. grew up in L.A., played blues and R&B in High School with the Soul Giants
2. became interested in music of **Edgard Varese** and Karlheinz Stockhausen
3. formed **Mothers of Invention** 1964

II. Musical Evolution: four phases

1. Freak Phase: 1966-1969 emphasized parody within acid rock multi-media events
    -   *Freak Out* 1967, first double album
    -   *Absolutely Free* 1967
    -   *We're Only In It For The Money* 1968 (Beatles satire)
    -   *Lumpy Gravy* 1968
    -   *Cruising With Reuben And The Jets* 1968
    -   *Uncle Meat* 1968 (use of unusual meters)
2. Jazz, Classical and Beyond: during period of hospitalization reevaluated career-began using more proficient sidemen in more serious musical statements
    -   *Hot Rats* 1969 (with Jean-Luc Ponty, violin)
    -   *Burnt Weeny Sandwich* (1970)
    -   *Weasels Ripped My Flesh* (1970)
    -   *Chunga's Revenge* 1970
3. Solo Focus 1976-1982: developed guitar technique featuring sophisticated solos within parodistic context
    -   *Joe's Garage* 1979
4. Techno Politics: 1982-1993 increased political activity (defending First Amendment Rights against PMRC); abandoned live performances increased use of synclavier, computer techniques
    -   *Jazz From Hell* 1986

III. Musical characteristics: eclectic mix of styles

1. use of recording technology important component of recordings
   - overdubbing, sampling
2. unusual or changing meters (Stravinsky)
3. electronic effects (Varese and Stockhausen)
   - musique concrete
4. free, often atonal improvisation
5. satire: mix of musical styles as well as politics
6. one of the first to stage mixed-media presentations (Freak Outs)

IV. Philosophical issues

1. personal freedom (influenced by Beats), distrust of government (censorship)
2. Iconoclast: attacked phony hippie conformity and drug use, pretentiousness of art-rock, lack of intellect in Punk

Selected Zappa Song List

1. Freak Out 1967:
   Hungry Freaks Daddy - political polemic
   Who Are The Brain Police - regimentation, electronics
   Go Cry On Somebody Else's Shoulder -doo wop parody
   Help I'm A Rock -extreme avant garde composition
2. Lumpy Gravy 1968 - most extreme concept album with 50 piece orch. stylistic juxtapositions
3. Crusin' With Reuben and the Jets 1968 - doo wop parody
   Cheap Thrills -anti romantic lyrics
   Love of My Life - parodies bass, triplets, falsetto, speaking text
4. Uncle Meat 1969: Stravinsky-Gamelan influenced, unusual time signatures
   The Voice of the Cheese (harpsichord transition to Suzie)
5. Hot Rats 1969 fusion jazz jams
   Willie The Pimp, Gumbo Variations
6. Sheik Yerbouti 1979: disco satire
   Dancing Fool
   Jewish Princess
7. Joes Garage Act 1 1979: Opera
   Wet Tee Shirt Night - scatalogical humor
   Why Does It Hurt When I Pee, Zappa Guitar solo
8. Ship Arriving Too Late to Save A Drowning Witch 1982
   Valley Girl, Zappa's biggest hit
9. Jazz From Hell 1986 synclavier electronics
   Jazz From Hell

Addenda: Short History of the Electric Guitar

I. Early Developments
1. *1931 Adolph Rickenbacker created first metal body guitar for Electro String Co.*
2. *Gibson introduced Charlie Christian pickup*
3. *Les Paul created new models in the 1940s*

II. Leo Fender: *Guitar genius*
1. *1948 Broadcaster (later called Telecaster), first commercially produced solid body guitar*
2. *1954 **Stratocaster**, featured 3 pickups, tremolo unit (first popularized by Buddy Holly)*
3. *Jazzmaster model*

III. Gibson models
1. *1952 Les Paul model*
2. *Les Paul Standard 1958-1960*
3. *Flying V 1959 (popularized by Bo Diddley)*

IV. Other models
1. *Kramer all aluminum neck*
2. *Gretsch (popularized by George Harrison)*
3. *Ibanez*
4. *Epiphone*

V. Amplifiers
1. *first tube amp max 10 watt range*
2. *1954 Fender Bassman Amp: 50 watts*
    Twin Reverb Amp contains 2 12 inch speakers
3. *Marshall Stack used in late 1960s: each amp contained 4 12-inch speakers enabled screeching and feedback, popularized by Pete Townshend (The Who)*
4. *1960 first transistor amps*

VI. Effects: *from the late 1960s guitar sounds were augmented by electronic effects*
1. *Echo (Echoplex) and Delay*
2. *Fuzz: overriding amp created tube distortion. Electro-Harmonia Big Muff distortion pedal popularized by Jimi Hendrix*
3. *Wah Wah pedal: Jen Cry Baby used by Hendrix*
4. *Phasing and Flanging*

VII. Bass Guitar
1. *Fender created precision bass guitar 1951, redesigned in 1957 and made popular by Carole Kaye and Duck Dunn (Booker and the MGs)*
2. *Hofner bass popularized by Paul McCartney*
3. *Fretless bass developed in 1970, popularized by Jaco Pastorious*

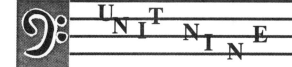
Conservative Reaction
(late 1960s - early 1970s)

Crosby, Stills, Nash and Young, 1974. UPI/CORBIS-BETTMANN.

As the decade of the 1960s came to a close, the idealism of the hippie experiment began to fade. With the growing escalation in Vietnam and Nixon's victory in 1968, the increasingly violent anti-war movement and the civil rights struggle were perceived as failures (see addenda). New kinds of folk and country rock emphasizing a softer, apolitical expression as well as the personal, introverted message of the singer-songwriters began to emerge. An important precursor to these developments were the post 1965 recordings of Bob Dylan.

Another return to basics style, southern rock, with its use of blues and soul featured a harder sound. An important recording company for country and southern rock was Capricorn Records, Macon Georgia, 1969-1979.

Addenda: Key Political Events of Anti-War Movement (1966-1970)

1965-1969: troop escalation in Vietnam 23,000 to 542,000
    1966: Univ. of Wisc. demonstrations over Dow chemical recruiting
    1967: large anti-war demonstrations in New York, San Francisco, Washington
    1968: Tet Offensive, Eugene McCarthy candidacy, Martin Luther King and Robert Kennedy
      assassinated, Riots at Democratic Convention in Chicago
    1969: Richard Nixon elected president. My Lai massacre, Manson family murders
      Woodstock and Altamount concerts, 100,000 members of SDS
    1970: Cambodian invasion. Four students killed at Kent State causes 508 major campus
      demonstrations Univ. of Wisc. Army Math Center bombing
      unemployment increased from 3.5% to 6.2%
    1973: peace treaty with North Vietnam, 56,555 American deaths
      drug related rock deaths: Brian Jones (1969) Janis Joplin, Jimi Hendrix (1970), Jim
      Morrison (1971)

I.   **Folk Rock:** important bands (mostly from L.A.)

    1.   **The Byrds** (David Crosby, Roger McGuinn, Michael Clarke, Chris Hellman): combined aspects of the Beatles and Dylan
-     *Mr. Tambourine Man* 1965
-     *Turn Turn Turn* 1966
-     *Fifth Dimension* 1966
-     *Eight Miles High*, more psychedelic, criticized for alleged drug reference
-     *The Notorious Byrd Bros.* 1968
-     Gram Parsons joined the band and introduced country style
      • *Sweetheart of the Rodeo* 1968

    2.   **Crosby, Stills, Nash** (and **Young**) superband noted for unique vocal harmony and strumming acoustic guitars, comprised of stars from other groups:
-     David Crosby (from the Byrds)
-     Stephen Stills (from Buffalo Springfield)
-     Graham Nash (from the Hollies)
-     and joining in 1969 Neil Young
-     number one album ***Deja Vu*** 1970 illustrates gamut of styles:
      • *Carry On*: acappella harmony, *Teach Your Children*: country (with Jerry Garcia), *4+20*: folk, *Woodstock* (written by Joni Mitchell): mainstream rock, *Helpless*: Neil Young's haunting ballad

    3.   Mamas And The Papas
-     hit singles *California Dreamin* 1966, *Monday, Monday* 1966, *Creeque Alley* 1967

II. Country Rock: important bands and performers

1. **Linda Ronstadt** (1946-) pop and country singer who added rock, mariachi, reggae mix to become crossover star of the 1970s
2. **Creedence Clearwater Revival** formed by John and Tom Fogerty, with its simple mix of rock and roll and country became the most popular band in America 1969 to 1970. Some of their hit singles (all from 1969) include:
    *   *Bad Moon Rising*
    *   *Proud Mary*
    *   *Born On The Bayou*
    *   *Down On The Corner*
3. **The Eagles** (Bernie Leadon, Glenn Frey, Don Henley, Randy Meisner, Don Felder) one-time backup band for Linda Ronstadt, the Eagles, with their mellow, slick sound became Southern California's most popular band of the 1970s
    *   best selling album: *Hotel California* 1976
4. **The Band** (Levon Helm, Garth Hudson, Robbie Robertson, Rich Danko, Richard Manuel, all from Canada except Helm) originally Bob Dylan's backup band
    *   albums: *Music From Big Pink* 1968
        The Band 1969
    *   hit single: *Up On Cripple Creek*
    -   1976: The Band made concert movie **The Last Waltz** directed by Martin Scorsese which included guest appearances by Eric Clapton, Bob Dylan, Joni Mitchell, Neil Young, Ringo Starr, Muddy Waters

III. Southern Rock: projecting the macho-outlaw good ol' boy stereotype, Southern Rock was a loud aggressive form of country rock combined with blues and soul that often featured twin dueling lead guitars and jazz-like improvisations.

1. **The Allman Bros.** (Duane Allman, Gregg Allman, Richard Betts, Jaimae Johanson, Butch Trucks) featured two lead guitars and two drummers reinterpreted British Blues in *Statesboro Blues* and jazz in *Whipping Post*
    -   double album hit: *At Fillmore East* 1971 features blues element
    -   1971 Duane Allman was killed in motorcycle crash
    -   later hit single: *Ramblin' Man* 1973
2. **Lynyrd Skynyrd**, from Jacksonville, Fla. utilized three lead guitars. Plane crash in 1977 killed three members of the band. Recordings include:
    *   *Free Bird* 1973
    *   *Sweet Home Alabama* 1974, recorded at Muscle Shoals
    *   *Swamp Music*
    *   *Needle and the Spoon*
    *   *Ballad of Curtis Loew*
    -   dance-oriented pieces usually open with bass riffs
3. **ZZ Top**: Texas based boogie power trio with Billy Gibbons, guitar, Dusty Hall, bass and Frank Beard, drums, formed in 1970
4. Charlie Daniels Band, led by country fiddler
5. Marshall Tucker Band

Singer-Songwriters

As a kind of second-generation Brill Building, songwriters reemerged in the 1970s as an important force in rock. Unlike the earlier composers, the new songwriters tended to perform their own music.

I. General Characteristics: (combined elements of 60s folk and pop)

1. self absorption, narcissism
2. semi-autobiographical confessional lyrics, often about pain of broken relationships
3. delicate 12-string acoustic guitar or piano accompaniment
4. appealed to urban, collegiate (proto-yuppie) audience

II. Important Singer-Songwriters

1. **James Taylor** (1948-) specialized in autobiographical songs. After recording in England helped define the genre in 1970 with album *Sweet Baby James* (with Carole King, piano) containing hit single, *Fire and Rain*

2. **Joni Mitchell** (Roberta Joan Anderson 1943-) Folk singer from Saskatoon created distinctive recitative-like vocals emphasizing highly sophisticated lyrics dealing with problems of interpersonal relationships. Later added elements of jazz and world music:
   - biggest hit: *Help Me* 1974

   albums include
   - *Court and Spark* 1974
   - *The Hissing of Summer Lawns* 1975
   - *Hejira* 1976
   - *Mingus* 1979

Joni Mitchell © Roger Ressmeyer/CORBIS

3. Carole King: Brill Building composer
   - *Tapestry* 1971, rock's first blockbuster album contained individual hits:
     • *I Feel The Earth Move, You've Got A Friend, A Natural Woman*
   - clean, uncluttered production by Lou Adler featured King's smooth R&B piano, strings, jazz harmonies
   - sold 13 million, in Top 40 for 65 weeks, won 4 Grammies, voted Album of the year
4. Carly Simon (1945-) biggest hit: *Anticipation* 1971
5. Billy Joel (1949-) pop pianist/composer whose career has extended into the 1990s
6. Don McClean: *American Pie* 1971- tribute to Buddy Holly and microcosm of rock history
7. Neil Young: *Harvest* 1972 with hit single *Heart of Gold*

Van Morrison

Evolving from R&B to a singer-songwriter comparable to Dylan or Neil Young but more eclectic and musically adventuresome, Northern Ireland's Van Morrison combines elements of blues, jazz, country, soul and Celtic elements. A private person, rarely granting interviews, Morrison has always felt the music should stand for itself without artificial studio effects, yet like most singer-songwriters, much of his work is autobiographical.

1. Born George Ivan Morrison in Belfast 1945. Father, a blue collar shipyard worker exposed Morrison to interesting record collection including Muddy Waters, Howlin' Wolf, Charlie Parker and trad. Celtic
2. Age 11 acquired guitar and began playing Skiffle with the "Sputniks"; began to play saxophone as a result of hearing Jimmy Giuffre records
3. 1960-61 playing in Irish horn based show bands. Read Kerouac and zen, start of life long interest in spirituality. Made living cleaning windows
   - "Cleaning Windows" (1982), autobiographical lyrics
   - 1962 formed "Monarchs", toured Scotland, Germany, moved to London
   - Began listening to Stones and Yardbirds
   - Begins composing
4. **THEM**, formed in 1964. Became one of Ireland's first R&B band. Many personnel changes
   - hits:
     • "Baby Please Don't Go" 1964
     • **"Gloria"** 1964 (first important Morrison original)
     • "Here Comes The Night" 1965
     • "Mystic Eyes" 1965 Bo-Diddleyesque original
5. Solo Career: moves to US
   • "Brown Eyed Girl" Calypso style, first solo hit
   - signs with Warner Bros.
6. **Astral Weeks** 1968 considered Morrison's most important album
   used jazz session players Richard Davis, bass, Connie Kay, drums
   • "Sweet Thing" acoustic guitar, syncopated bass, bkg strings
   - lives in Woodstock, NY, hangs out with the Band
7. **Moondance** most popular album, used soul and jazz
   • "Moondance" modal jazz with flute
   • "And It Stoned Me" shows Country Rock influence of the Band
8. **Domino** 1970 using Stax-like soul horns, became Morrison's best selling single
9. Begins to explore Celtic music and forms the Caldonian Soul Orchestra
   • "I'll Tell Me Ma" 1988

Blockbuster Albums (late 1970s)

I. **Fleetwood Mac:** British band that combined Blues and Country Rock was great popular success in mid to late 1970s:

- *Rumors* 1977 sold 17 million with hit single *Go Your Own Way*

II. **Peter Frampton:**

- *Frampton Comes Alive* 1976 sold 10 million

Corporate Rock: The Majors Take Over

During the 1970s the record business was taken over by corporate America, starting a trend that will increase with the advent of MTV in 1981.

I. **By the mid 1970s** the recording industry was dominated by seven major conglomerates:

1.	CBS	4.	Polygram	7.	Warner Communications
2.	Capitol	5.	RCA		(who will start MTV 1981)
3.	MCA	6.	A&M		

II. **Growth of recording industry:**

1950	1971	1978
$189 million	$1.7 billion	$4 billion

- by 1975, rock accounted for 80% of all record sales

III. **Profits** came from around the world: 1973 sales figures included:

- $2 billion sold in U.S. $555 million Japan, $454 million West Germany
- $441 million Soviet Union, $384 million Britain

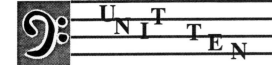
Funk and Jazz Rock (1970s)

Sly & the Family Stone, 1968. UPI/CORBIS-BETTMANN.

With the assassination of Martin Luther King Jr. and the failures of the civil rights movement, some African-American music turned from the integrated sounds of Mo-Town and STAX, and modeled on the late 60s recordings of James Brown, began evolving Funk, an uncompromising inner-city musical style distinct from mainstream White America. Elements of Funk were adopted by jazz musicians to create the Fusion, or Jazz-Rock style. Near the end of the 1970s, the new dance craze Disco, based on simplified funk rhythms, emerged. Parallel to this was the development of film and TV shows specifically designed for Black audiences (see addenda).

I. Musical Characteristics of Funk (many showing influence of James Brown):

1. emphasis on rhythm over melody or harmony
2. rhythm section instruments prominent, especially bass
3. horns (saxes and trumpets) used for riffs, not melodies
4. conversational chanting vocal style derived from gospel
5. polyrhythmic layering

II. Important bands and performers

1. **Sly Stone** (Sylvester Stewart 1944-) San Francisco D.J. created a commercially successful blend of funk and acid rock
   - 1966 formed Sly and the Family Stone, an integrated and intergender band featured bassist Larry Graham's percussive "pops"
   - important recordings after 1969 Woodstock appearance:
     • *Thank You (Falettineme Be Mice Elf Again)*
     • *Family Affair*
     • *There's A Riot Goin On*

2. **George Clinton** (1944-) first worked at Mo-Town formed Parliaments, then 1968 Funkadelic, sometimes called Parliament
   - featured Sci-Fi and comic book glitter personae with elaborate stage presentations, bassist Bootsie Collins, saxophonist Maceo Parker important ex-James Brown sidemen
   - breakthrough album: *Mothership Connection* 1974, followed by
     • *The Clones Of Dr. Funkenstein* 1976
     • *Funkentelechy Vs. The Placebo Syndrome* 1977
     • *Flash Light* 1978

Stevie Wonder © Henry Dilz/CORBIS

3. **Stevie Wonder** after his break with Mo-Town released a series of commercial and artistically acclaimed albums which created a jazz-flavored funk:
   • *My Cherie Amor, You Are The Sunshine of My Life*, Latin-flavored hits

- *Superstition* (1973) popularized clavinet
- ***Innervisions*** 1973 (featuring *Living In The City*)
- double album: *Songs In The Key Of Life* 1976
- *Journey Through The Secret Life Of Plants* 1979
- Characteristics:
  - helped define synthesizer usage
  - studio recording techniques (plays all the instruments on Innervision)
  - sophisticated jazz harmony
  - Latin influences
4. **Kool And The Gang**, founded in 1968 created danceable funk.
   - hit single: *Funky Stuff* 1973
5. **Earth, Wind and Fire**: pop mainstream funk, combined astrology with commerce

III. Later Funk of the 1980s:

1. Average White Band, from Scotland
2. Red-Hot-Chili Peppers
3. Fishbone

Addenda: Black Oriented Film and TV in the 1970s

1971: Shaft, directed by Gordon Parks Jr. with music by STAX writer Isaac Hayes, first Hollywood Blaxpoitation film
TV Sitcom: The Jeffersons
1972: Superfly, directed by Parks and music by Curtis Mayfield. Depiction of cocaine dealer concerned NAACP
1973: Enter The Dragon: Bruce Lee's first Kung-Fu movie, while not all-Black cast, was aimed at Black market.
The Harder They Come, starring Jimmy Cliff, helps launch Reggae craze.
1975: Cooley High, depicts growing up in Chicago housing project.
TV sitcom: Good Times
1977: Alex Haley's Roots TV miniseries generates highest ratings for network program.
1979: Richard Pryor's Live In Concert.

Fusion/Jazz Rock

Attracted by the technological accomplishments of Rock as well as being lured by its commercial potential, some jazz musicians began incorporating elements of funk into a post be-bop jazz style to create fusion, or jazz-rock. At the same time, many rock players were attracted to the greater complexity and sophistication of jazz with its emphasis on improvisation.

I. Elements of fusion taken from rock:

1. use of recording studio techniques
2. use of electronic keyboards and electric bass guitar
3. straight-8th note rock rhythm in drums combined with repetitive bass lines
4. horns used for riffs and background vamps

II. Elements of complexity retained from jazz:

1. instrumental rather than vocal
2. virtuoso improvisation, sometimes using avant garde techniques
3. harmony generally more complex
4. longer compositions, sometimes stream of consciousness approach

III. Importance of Miles Davis:

1. helped launch career of many fusionists:
   - pianists: Herbie Hancock, Chick Corea, Keith Jarrett
   - guitar: John McLaughlin, John Scofield
   - saxophone: Cannonball Adderley, Wayne Shorter, Bennie Maupin, Steve Grossman, Bill Evans
   - bass: Ron Carter, Dave Holland, Marcus Miller
   - drums: Tony Williams, Jack DeJohnette, Billy Cobham
2. influential 1969 jazz-rock recordings:
   - *In A Silent Way*
   - *Bitches Brew*

IV. Four important jazz-influenced pop-rock bands of the late 1960s:

1. **Electric Flag**: formed in 1967 by Mike Bloomfield, Buddy Miles, et al.
   - last album before breakup: *Electric Flag* 1969
2. **Blood, Sweat, and Tears**: dominated by jazz horn improvisations and sophisticated arrangements
   - *Child Is Father Of The Man*
   - *Blood, Sweat, And Tears 1969* #1 album
   - *Blood, Sweat, And Tears* 1970 #1
3. **Chicago** (originally Chicago Transit Authority), managed and marketed by James Guercio. Combined rock rhythm section with jazz horns (trpt, sax, tbn.)
   - created very successful pop jazz rock series of double albums:
     - *Chicago Transit Authority* 1969 # 17
     - *Chicago II* 1970 #4
     - *Chicago III* 1971#2
     - *Chicago V* 1972, *Chicago VI* 1973, *Chicago VIII* 1974, *Chicago VIIII* 1975 all #1
   - In 1975, lead guitarist and principle soloist Terry Kath, accidentally shot to death
4. **Steeley Dan**, formed in 1973 by Donald Fagan and Walter Becker
   - *Pretzel Logic* 1974

V. Important instrumental fusion bands of the 1970s comprised of jazz players turning to rock:

1. **Herbie Hancock**'s Headhunters: multi-layered African inspired rhythms
   - *Watermelon Man* 1974
   - *Thrust* 1974, influenced by Sly
2. **Weather Report**: co led by Joe Zawinul and Wayne Shorter created tight, complex ensemble pieces. Featured bass virtuoso Jaco Pastorious
   - 1977 album *Heavy Weather*, contained hit single *Birdland*
3. Return To Forever: led by keyboardist **Chick Corea** created a smooth sophisticated blend of rock, jazz, classical, latin
   - *Light As A Feather* 1973
4. **John McLaughlin** (guitar) and the **Mahavishnu Orchestra**: added elements of Indian music:
   - *Birds Of Fire* 1973
   - *Apocalypse* (with the London Symphony) 1974
   - *Shakti* (with violinist L.Shankar)

Addenda: The Development of Electronic Keyboards (1960-1980)

I.   Organ
   *1. 1939 **Hammond** Organ (designed by Laurene Hammond) introduced, model B-3 becomes favorite. Popularized by Jimmy Smith, Booker T. and Keith Emerson (from Emerson, Lake and Palmer)*
   2. Leslie Organ speaker crated tremolo through phasing of speakers

II.   Mellotron *(Mel ody +elec tronics)*
   1. created in Birmingham, England 1963
   2. used by Beatles, especially on Strawberry Fields Forever 1967
   3. model 400 most popular, appeared in 1970

III. Electric Piano
   1. Wurlitzer EP 2000, appeared in 1960
   *2. Fender-**Rhodes** (Rhodes) became popular late 1960s. Featured several different models, from 88 to 73 keys, in Stage or Suitcase models. Popularized by Chick Corea, Herbie Hancock*
   3. Hohner Clavinet: popularized by Stevie Wonder

IV. Analog Monophonic Synthesizers
   *1. 1964: Robert **Moog** creates first commercial electronic synthesizer. several different models including portable Mini-Moog and Micro-Moog*
   2. other brands included Arp Odyssey, Putney, Roland, Korg

V.   Specialized Synthesizers
   1. polyphonic (capable of playing chords) String Synthesizer
   2. Drum machines

VI. Later digital synthesizers
   1. Yamaha DX 7 and other models. became keyboard of choice in the 1980s
   2. sequencers

VII. MIDI *(Music Instrument Digital Interface)*

VIII. Sampling: *recreating acoustic sounds with computer*

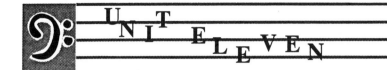

Heavy Metal Glam/Glitter (1970s)

Robert Plant and Jimmy Page of "Led Zeppelin." REUTERS/CORBIS-BETTMANN.

A new, loud, aggressive form of blues-derived music began to be developed in Britain in the late 1960s as an alternative to the Beatles and art rock. These younger bands drew inspiration from the Rolling Stones, The Who, and Jimi Hendrix. While representing a return to basics theme, both Hard Rock, with more of a blues emphasis, and Heavy Metal pioneered guitar technology emphasizing high volume, distortion and feedback. Metal can be divided into two phases, the first, featuring mostly British bands, and a second, smoother version beginning in the mid 1970s featuring both British and American bands. Later forms of Metal continue to be popular.

Metal

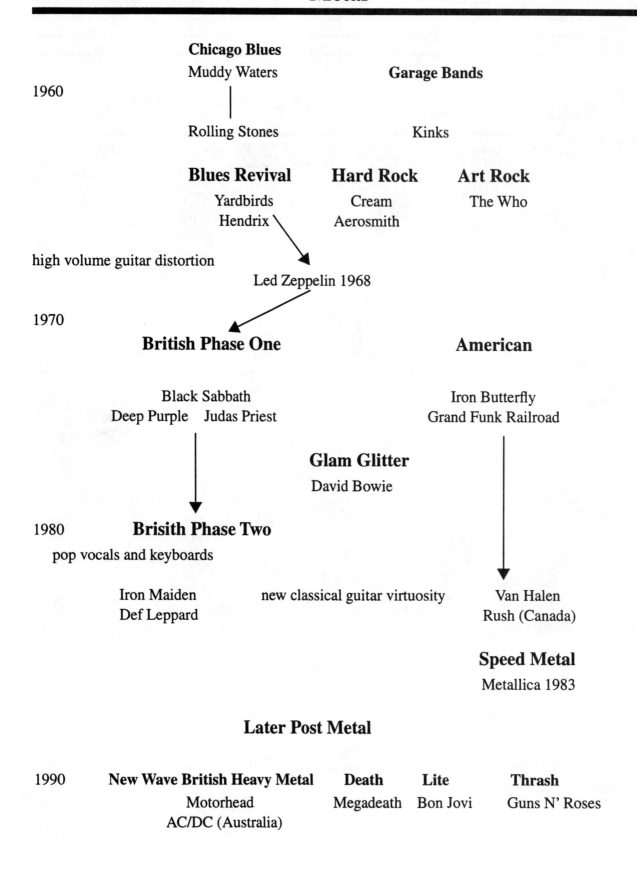

Chicago Blues

Muddy Waters

Garage Bands

1960

Rolling Stones

Kinks

Blues Revival   **Hard Rock**   **Art Rock**

Yardbirds   Cream   The Who

Hendrix   Aerosmith

high volume guitar distortion

Led Zeppelin 1968

1970

British Phase One   **American**

Black Sabbath   Iron Butterfly

Deep Purple   Judas Priest   Grand Funk Railroad

Glam Glitter

David Bowie

1980   **Brisith Phase Two**

pop vocals and keyboards

Iron Maiden   new classical guitar virtuosity   Van Halen

Def Leppard   Rush (Canada)

Speed Metal

Metallica 1983

Later Post Metal

1990   **New Wave British Heavy Metal**   **Death**   **Lite**   **Thrash**

Motorhead   Megadeath   Bon Jovi   Guns N' Roses

AC/DC (Australia)

I. Characteristics:

1. identified with violence and aggression, aimed at teen, male audience
2. LOUD: necessary for large stadiums venues
3. use of guitar distortion, feedback and other noise effects
4. extended improvisations including long drum solos
5. linked to Glam/Glitter with elaborate stage presentations
6. use of gothic themes of medieval castles and torture as well as satanic glorification of evil, black magic, witchcraft, and death
7. recordings created for AOR (album oriented FM radio) format
8. generally depicted by critics in negative terms: testosterone-driven, raw, unrefined, sluggish, lumbering, anti-social, misogynistic
9. criticized for dependence on technology: tending to create machine-like uniformity of sound, exaggerated effects over musical substance

II. Hard Rock forerunners: ("blues on steroids")

1. **Cream (Eric Clapton**, guitar, Jack Bruce, bass, Ginger Baker, drums): power trio
   featured blues-influenced guitar, repeating bass lines and powerful drumming (using two bass drums)
   - albums include:
     - *Disraeli Gears* 1967
     - *Wheels of Fire* 1968
2. Steppenwolf: formed in 1967
   - *Born To Be Wild* 1968 (uses words *Heavy Metal* in lyrics), featured in film *Easy Rider*
3. Aerosmith: formed in Boston 1970
   - *Sweet Emotion*
   - *Walk This Way* (later covered by Run DMC)

III. Led Zeppelin (**Jimmy Page** guitar, **Robert Plant** vocal, John Bonham (aka Bonzo) drums, John Paul Jones bass, most important band in development of Metal.

1. formed by Page (from the Yardbirds) and Plant in 1968
2. 1970 ousted Beatles as Britain's most popular band
3. by 1973 most popular rock band in the world:
   - *Led Zeppelin* 1969 included Willie Dixon covers, *Communication Breakdown, Dazed and Confused* using bass riff
   - *Led Zeppelin II* 1969 included *Whole Lotta Love, Moby Dick,* drum feature
   - *Led Zeppelin III* 1970, with Celtic Bron-Y-Aur Stomp
   - *Led Zeppelin IV* (or *Zo-So*) 1971 included **Stairway To Heaven** and *Black Dog*
   - *Houses Of The Holy* 1973
   - *Physical Graffiti* 1975, with *Kashmir* influenced by Indian raga
4. several tours of America created anti-establishment image
5. some specific musical characteristics:
   - early tunes based on bass riffs, later used Celtic folk material
   - use occult material (Aleister Crowley)
   - Page: avoided clean sound, preferred muddy distortion, invented bowed guitar
   - Plant: high voice range with distorted screams and howls
   - Bonham: incredibly loud, active drums
   - engineered with reverb, echo, and emphasis on bass and bass drum
   - songs often start soft building to climax of volume and violence
   - unlike many Metal bands, did not use Glam/glitter productions

6. influence began to decline 1975, with the group disbanding after Bonham's death in 1980
    *   *Presence* 1976
    *   *The Song Remains The Same* 1976 (film soundtrack)

IV. British Metal Phase One early 1970s:

1. Black Sabbath: first true Metal Band, featured vocalist Ozzy Osbourne until 1978, "Doom/Death Metal" used occult themes
    influenced Megadeth, Twisted Sister, AC/DC, Motorhead
2. Deep Purple: flirted with art rock before going metal in the early 1970s *Smoke on the Water*
3. Judas Priest: marketed as biker tough guy image, featured two lead guitarists in the debut album:
    *   *Rocka Rolla* 1974
    -   continued as one of the dominant British metal band on the 1980s

V. British Metal Phase Two: late 1970s-1980s: more pop oriented, added keyboards.

1. **Iron Maiden**: projected satanic image of torture and death, sang through vocal enhancers
2. **Def Leppard**: by early 1980s had perfected pop-metal escapism with tight vocal harmonies singing unobtrusive lyrics. Career peaked with release of third album:
    *   *Pyromania* 1983
    -   band declined after accident to drummer Rick Allen in 1987 and death of guitarist Steve Clark in 1991

Metallica © S.I.N./CORBIS

VI. American Metal: tended to be lighter and more melodic than British.

1. Iron Butterfly: early California Metal
   - *In-A-Gadda-Da-Vida* 1968 featured 17-min cut
2. Grand Funk Railroad: debuted before 100,000 at 1969 Atlanta Pop Festival
3. **Van Halen**: formed by **Eddie** and Alex **Van Halen** in 1974, created a smoother, polished style characterized by shorter, virtuosic guitar solos of Eddie and David Lee Roth vocals, replaced in 1985 by Sammy Hagar
   - originally trained as a pianist, Eddie Van Halen used classical techniques (two-handed hammering and harmonics) to redefine a new, sophisticated guitar style
   - released first album in 1978 followed by *Van Halen II* 1979
4. Rush: Canadian power trio, added synthesizers and elements of art rock with multi-movement forms and unusual meters
   - *Fly By Night* 1975
5. **Metallica**: California based band led in developing Speed Metal:
   - debut album *Kill 'Em All* 1983
     - *Master Of Puppets* 1986
     - *And Justice For All* 1988
     - *Metallica* 1991
   - featured long virtuosic tunes
   - higher ratio of instrumental-to-vocal
   - guitar-based, rejection of keyboards as pop elements
   - non-traditional harmony modes or drones (raga rock) instead
   - remains among most popular bands of the 1990s

VII. Later Metal Styles:

1. Thrash Metal (or Speed Metal) combined elements of Punk
   - Anthrax
2. Post Metal:
   - Bon Jovi: formed in 1983 by Jon Bon Jovi (John Bongiovi) darlings of MTV ("Hair Band")
   - Guns N' Roses, led by guitarist Slash and lead singer Axl Rose
   - Queensrÿche, from Seattle
3. New Wave British Heavy Metal (NWBHM)
   - Motorhead
   - AC/DC (from Australia)
   - Motley Crue

Glam/Glitter: Rock as Theater

The Glam/Glitter movement, with its theatrical emphasis on visual spectacle, sexual freedom expressed by androgynous (bisexual) figures, and a generally lack of interest in social/political issues, emerged as the self-indulgent decade of the 1970s reaction to the hippie subculture of the 1960s. Extravagant musical forces, essentially using a musical style composed of Heavy Metal with elements of art rock, placed more emphasis on the production and stressed the dramatic personality of the lead singer (performance artist) rather than his/her musicianship. Like Metal, the Glam/Glitter movement first emanated from style-conscious London with the work of David Bowie and Elton John.

I. **David Bowie** (David Jones 1947-) influenced by Dylan, Andy Warhol, Lou Reed, Oscar Wilde, pioneered in theatrical glam/glitter rock, master at manipulating audiences with stage personas.

1. background as a commercial artist, studied mime and acting
2. 1967 first folk-rock band: David Jones and The Lower Third projected haughty, upper class persona
3. influenced by manager Tony De Fries, changed name to David Bowie openly declared his bisexuality and began performing as androgyene
4. 1968 appears as Major Tom in *Space Oddity*, popularized by BBC during moon landing
5. 1970 first American appearance: dressed as drag queen, with elaborate makeup influenced by Japanese Kabuki
6. important albums:
   - *Hunky Dory* 1972
   - *The Rise And Fall Of Ziggy Stardust* 1973
   - *Spider Man From Mars* 1972 projected extraterrestrial persona
   - *Alladin Sane* 1973
   - *Diamond Dogs* 1974
7. period of tours using complex and ornate sets (1974 Diamond Dogs Tour set cost $250,000)
8. turned to acting career:
   - play: *The Elephant Man*
   - film: *The Man Who Fell To Earth*

II. Elton John (Reginald Kenneth Dwight 1947-) brought the piano pyrotechnics of Little Richard and Jerry Lee Lewis to Glitter.

1. Raised in London as piano prodigy, 1964 first band: Bluesology
2. 1967 met lyricist Bernie Taupin, began collaborating with under the nom de plume Elton John. Taupin/John began cranking out eclectic pop rock influenced by PIR
3. First American tour 1970, becomes famous for flamboyant dress (especially $40,000 worth of glasses) and outrageous stage antics
4. First album: *Empty Sky*, first American album: Elton John 1970
5. During the mid-1970s Elton John became the preeminent performer in rock with a string of seven number one hit albums:
   - *Honkey Chateau* 1972
   - *Don't Shoot Me I'm Only The Piano Player* 1973
   - *Goodby Yellowbrick Road* 1973
   - *Caribou* 1974
   - *Captain Fantastic And The Brown Dirt Cowboy* 1975
   - *Rock Of The Westies* 1975

III. Other important British theatrical rock bands

1. Marc Bolan (Marc Field 1948-1977) and T. Rex, influenced by Bowie, used softer, acoustic folk rock
2. Roxy Music, with Brian Eno, synthesizer and Bryan Ferry
3. Mott the Hoople, led by Ian Hunter: another Bowie-influenced band projected gay image
4. **Rod Stewart** (1945-): began touring America in 1970 with The Faces moved from workingman's image to spandex glam stardom:
   - hit single: *Maggie Mae* 1971
   - albums: *Every Picture Tells A Story* 1971
     Never A Dull Moment 1972
     Smiler 1974
     Atlantic Crossing 1975
5. Queen: androgynous hard rock: *Bohemian Rhapsody* 1975 shows classical operatic influence

IV. American Glam:

1. **Alice Cooper** (Vincent Fournier 1945-) combined occult (name taken from Ouija board) and horror (used live snakes)
   - best selling albums: *School's Out* 1972
     Billion Dollar Babies 1973
     Muscle Of Love 1973
2. **Kiss**: NY based Metal band used horror movie images to target young audience. Stage personas important (for 12 years were never photographed without makeup)

V. Black Glam: George Clinton (see page 54)

Disco

Near the end of the 1970s the relentless rhythms of Disco (from discotheque) became the latest dance craze in America. Derived from simplified funk patterns and influenced by the European synthesizer band Kraftwerk, Disco originally was associated with the New York Latin and African American gay scene. By using recorded music exclusively, Disco shifted the center of attention away from the musicians to the dancers and DJs. Night clubs, such as Studio 54 in New York, Zorine's in Chicago, and Dillion's in Los Angeles featuring many-tiered strob-lit rooms that became chic meeting places for celebrities and wanabes. No form of music has been more universally condemned by musicians than Disco.

I. Discomania

1. 1977: *Saturday Night Fever*, starring John Travolta, sound track by the Bee Gees sold 30 million
2. 1978: 20,000 discos in America (Holiday Inn added 35 Discos to its chain)
   - Disco accounted for 20% of all releases
3. 1979: disco had become a $5 billion industry

II. Some social characteristics:

1. starting in gay clubs, became focal point of gay liberation
2. disco culture associated with cocaine
3. unrestrained sexuality in dance
4. glitter attire
5. DJ becomes species of pop artist

III. Musical characteristics: mechanical rhythmic background

1. smooth Black urban dance pop reflecting PIR, funk, Isaac Hayes influence
2. throbbing, insistent funky bass-driven pulse in unsyncopated 4/4
3. prominent use of synthesizers
4. European disco (Eurodisco) featured long pieces filling up entire albums sides without breaks

IV. Important groups and performers:

1. The Village People: multi-racial gay ensemble
2. KC and the Sunshine Band (led by Harry Casey and Richard Finch)
   - hit singles: *Get Down Tonight* and *That's The Way I Like It* 1975
3. **Bee Gees**: Australian family band (Robin, Maurice, and Barry Gibb)
   - Saturday Night Fever with hit single *Stayin Alive* 1977
4. Giorgio Moroder (1941-): king of Eurodisco, influence on Techno

5.   **Donna Summer** (1948-): trained as Gospel singer, first worked in Europe with Moroder: notorious for orgiastic moaning
- *Love To Love You Baby* 1975
- *MacArthur Park Suite* 1978
- *Hot Stuff* 1979

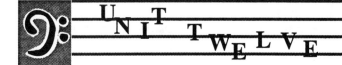
Punk—The Underground Fights Back (late 1970s)

Sid Vicious and Johnny Rotten of the "Sex Pistols," 1978. UPI/CORBIS-BETTMANN.

Reaching its peak in the late 1970s, Punk Rock, the inevitable grass roots reaction to the excesses of Metal and Glam combined the dilettantism of the garage band with cutting edge avant garde of the art world. Beginning in New York, a more radical form of Punk emerged in Britain, and by the end of the decade, New Wave, a more mainstream form of Punk became popular. In addition to a musical style, Punk, performed almost exclusively by Whites, represented a counter-culture, anti-establishment attitude (similar to early Rock & Roll) by attempting to eliminate the distinction between audience and performer by purposeful casual dressing and deemphasizing musical technical proficiency.

81

Punk to Alternative

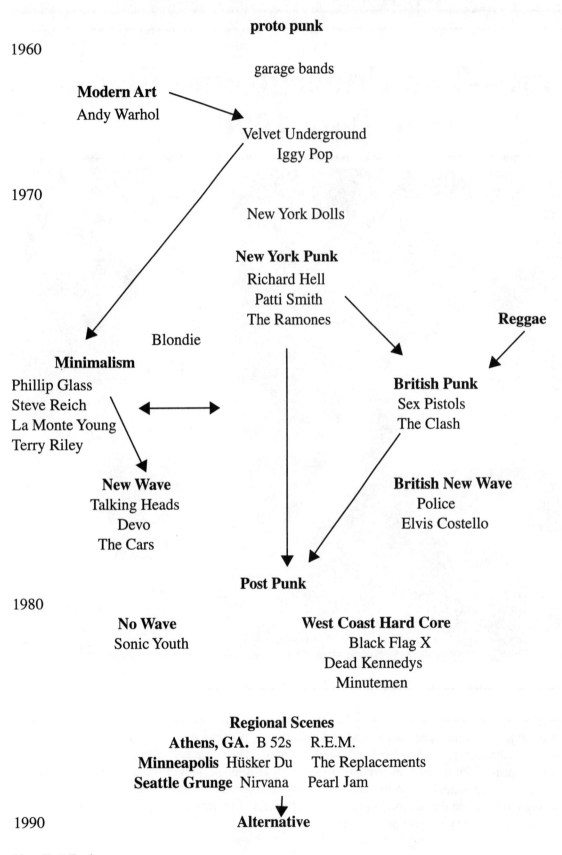

proto punk

1960

garage bands

Modern Art
Andy Warhol

Velvet Underground
Iggy Pop

1970

New York Dolls

New York Punk
Richard Hell
Patti Smith
The Ramones

Reggae

Blondie

Minimalism
Phillip Glass
Steve Reich
La Monte Young
Terry Riley

British Punk
Sex Pistols
The Clash

New Wave
Talking Heads
Devo
The Cars

British New Wave
Police
Elvis Costello

Post Punk

1980

No Wave
Sonic Youth

West Coast Hard Core
Black Flag X
Dead Kennedys
Minutemen

Regional Scenes
Athens, GA. B 52s   R.E.M.
Minneapolis Hüsker Du   The Replacements
Seattle Grunge Nirvana   Pearl Jam

Alternative

1990

Influence of Modern Art

Part of early American Punk was influenced by the Avant Garde Art scene in New York, especially Pop art and Andy Warhol.

I. European Art Movements 1910-1940

1. Dada: radical nihilistic philosophy began as reaction to World War I. questioned and ridiculed values of Art. Used improvisation and chance
   - important artists: Marcel du Champ, Man Ray,
2. Surrealism: invoked the fantasy world of dreams
   - Salvidore Dali, Max Ernst
3. Abstract: replaced representational objects with shape and color
   - phase one - organic shapes: Vassily Kandinsky, Paul Klee,
   - phase two - geometric grids: Piet Mondrian (emigrated to America 1940)

II. American Art Movement 1940s-1970

1. Abstract Expressionism: various styles influenced by Europe. Became mainstream style in the 1950s
   - Jackson Pollack, Willem de Kooning, Mark Rothko
2. Pop: using common objects as subjects for art
   - Jasper Johns (flags, targets) **Andy Warhol** (soup cans) Roy Lichtenberg (cartoons)

III. Importance of **John Cage** (1912-1992) composer whose ideas have influenced the arts and philosophy:

1. used sound-noise (late 1930s), silence (1952), as music
2. used chance procedures (I Ching) in composing process (1951)
3. among the first to create electronic music (1950s)
4. helped popularize Eastern philosophies (Zen) (1940s)
5. introduced the multi-media happening (1952)

Punk (Name Derived From New York Fanzine)

I. Proto-Punk:

The Velvet Underground formed by **Lou Reed**, guitar-vocals, and violist **John Cale**, with Sterling Morrison, guitar and Maureen Tucker, drums. In 1965 became part of Andy Warhol's "Exploding Plastic Inevitable" and laid the foundations for later Punk:

- combined the pop sensibilities of Reed with the experimental avant garde of Cale
- repetitive 8th-note ostinatos and drones
- shouted vocals (anti vocals)
- trealistic songs reflecting NY street life with themes of alienation, drug use and sadomasochism

1. Four Studio Recordings (none of which cracked the top 100):
   - *The Velvet Underground & Nico* 1966, released 1967 with cover art (banana) by Warhol (with Sterling Morrison, guitar, Maureen Tucker, drums and Nico, vocals, included:
   - *Waiting for the Man* (Reed): relentless ostinato
   - *Femme Fatale*: written specifically for Nico
   - *Heroin*: features changing tempos and viola dissonances

- *Venus in Furs*: S&M text with viola drone
  - *White Light/White Heat* 1968 dominated by Cale's use of noise and distortion including *Sister Ray*

Cale leaves, replaced by Doug Yule, bass
  - *The Velvet Underground* 1969, introspective songs like Reed's *Pale Blue Eyes*
  - *Loaded* 1970

The Legacy of the Velvets

Although never a commercial popular success, the Velvet Underground had a direct influence on later musicians such as Brian Eno, David Bowie, Patti Smith, Iggy Pop, Chrisse Hynde, and bands like R.E.M., U2, Joy Division, Sonic Youth, The Cars, and The Talking Heads.

II. Other early bands

1. Iggy (James Osterberg) and the Stooges: while student at Univ. of Michigan, Iggy played drums in The Iguanas. formed own band in 1967 used stage diving, self-mutilation and violence.
   - John Cale produced first album: *The Stooges* 1969
2. The New York Dolls: transvestite band formed in 1971, managed by Malcolm McLaren
   - made two albums:
     - *The New York Dolls* 1973
     - *Too Much Too Soon* 1974
3. The Dictators: archtypical garage band *Cars and Girls* 1975

III. New York Punk: the importance of CBGB (Country, Blue Grass, Blues) 1975 began featuring Punk bands. 1975 CBGB Rock Festival Showcase Auditions (featuring Ramones, Talking Heads, Television) drew national attention to burgeoning Punk scene.

1. **Patti Smith** (1946-) poetry influenced by beats
   - first album produced by John Cale: *Horses* 1975

Patti Smith © Owen Franken/CORBIS

2. Television, and **Richard Hell**, (Richard Meyers) whose Punk dress and hair style was widely imitated (short, brightly-dyed spiked hair, torn tee-shirt, various pierced body parts)
3. **The Ramones**, formed in 1974, each member changed last name to Ramone (after a Paul McCartney pseudonym): high energy style with buzz-saw guitar sound, less interested in avant garde, their tour of England in 1976 helped start British Punk
   - *Ramones* 1976 (recorded for $6000)
   - one of the few original punk bands still active
4. Blondie (with Debbie Harry)

IV. **British Punk:** angry, more desperate than American, reflected boredom and anger of unemployed youths, influenced by Reggae. Because of its volatile nature, most British Punk was recorded on independent, underground labels.

1. **The Sex Pistols** Johnny Rotten (John Lydon), **Sid Vicious** (John Ritchie), Paul Cook, Steve Jones: promoted by Malcolm McLaren, owner of Sex, a counter-culture clothing store, played first show 1975.
   - influenced by NY Dolls and Ramones
   - singles *Anarchy in the U.K.* and *God Save The Queen* released in 1977 to coincide with Queen Elizabeth's Silver Jubilee although banned from radio/television became popular album:
     - *Never Mind The Bullocks* became # 1
   - tours of Europe and US, 1978 Vicious died of drug overdose
2. **The Clash**: comprised of more professional musicians
   criticized for signing with CBS records
     - *London Calling* 1980 double album, including *Guns of Brixton* using Reggae

V. **West Coast Hardcore Punk:** influenced by British

1. Dead Kennedys: formed in San Francisco in 1978
2. two Los Angeles bands:
   - Black Flag: influenced by Sex Pistols
   - X, formed in 1977, produced by Doors' Ray Manzarek, featured Doe and Exene Cervenka chanting

Reactions Against Punk

Like early Rock & Roll, Punk has been severely criticized by the establishment:

- the most left-wing of the contemporary groups *The British Patriot*
- All that punk singers can bring to the presentation of their songs is the gesture of sexual obscenity or of impotent rage *Anthony Burgess*
- punk rock is the generic term for the latest musical garbage bred by our troubled children. It features screaming, venomous, threatening sounds *London Times*
- the Sex Pistols do as much for music as World War II did for the cause of peace. *Melody Maker*
- Punk is so constipated it should be called hemorrhoid rock. *Linda Ronstadt*

Importance of Punk

While never achieving the popularity of other rock styles, punk was important in that it rearticulated the historic role of rock as a youthful reaction to the status quo. It cleared the air of the excesses of Glam/Glitter and disco and has continued to exert an influence on later music. The so-called alternative of the 1980s and 90s owe much to the legacy of punk as does some aspects of mainstream superstars like Madonna, and Michael Jackson, and in a larger context, the look and philosophy of punk affected a whole generation of adolescents.

New Wave

The New Wave of the late 1970s, by commercializing and toning down some of the more sensational aspect of Punk, reached a larger, mainstream audience. Keeping the chant-like ostinati vocals and incessant rhythms of Punk, New Wave used keyboards and other instruments to create a clearer, slicker sound. Much of New Wave was influenced by the avant garde music of Philip Glass, Steve Reich, Terry Riley and others called **Minimalism**. Reggae was also used, especially with British groups.

I. **Minimalism** (or systematic music): avant garde classical music that both influenced and was influenced by New Wave, featured a constant repetitive beat with slowly changing melodies during which compositional processes gradually unfold.

1. Philip Glass: studied with Ravi Shankar, interacted with New Wave
   opera premiered at the Met:
   - *Einstein On The Beach* 1976
2. Steve Reich: studied Indian drumming, created phase music
   - *Come Out* 1966
   - *Four Organs*
3. Terry Riley: influenced by Eastern religion
   - *Sri Camel* uses non-western scale tuning
4. La Monte Young: worked with John Cale

II. **American New Wave**

1. **Devo** formed by Kent State students Mark Mothersbaugh and Jerry Casale:
   - specialized in unemotional, robot-like electronic songs:
     - *Q: Are we not men? A: We Are Devo!* 1976
2. **Talking Heads**: formed by Rhode Island School of Design students David Byrne, Chris Frantz, and Tina Weymouth, eccentric, tense
3. The Cars: *Door To Door* 1987

III. **British New Wave**

1. **Elvis Costello** (Declan MacManus 1955-) influenced by Buddy Holly before adding reggae and punk
   - formed the Attractions in 1978
     - *Red Shoes* 1977
     - *Veronica* 1989 (with Paul McCartney)
2. Billy Idol: left Generation X in 1981 and moved to more pop sound
   - *Rebel Yell* 1983
3. Adam Ant (Stewart Goddard) and the Ants 1980-1985
   - *Kings Of The Wild Frontier*
4. **The Police** led by **Sting** (Gordon Summer) bass, Stewart Copeland, drums, Andy Summers (guitar):
   - used reggae and jazz: *Roxanne* 1977 hit single
   Synchronicity 1983, includes:
   - *Synchronicity:* ostinato
   - *Walking in Your Footsteps*; Calypso

-    *Miss Gradenko*; reggae
-    *Every Breath You Take*; ballad with ostinato

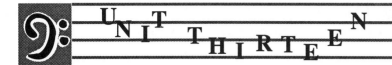

Rap

Run DMC © Lynn Goldsmith/CORBIS

Rap and Hip Hop arose out of the need for a musical language that would reflect life in the urban African-American community (see addenda). In some respects, Rap can be seen as following in the tradition of Black music from R&B, Soul, and Funk combined with the technological advances of the 1980s and strongly influenced by Reggae. Some of Rap's more outspoken political messages (Gangsta Rap) have been criticized by the White establishment. The rapper's response is that they are functioning as reporters of the social condition, telling it like it is. While the terms are somewhat synonymous, hip hop is often used to describe the larger street culture including graffiti art, clothing styles and break dancing while rap refers to a later, more politicized form of music.

Hip Hop to Rap

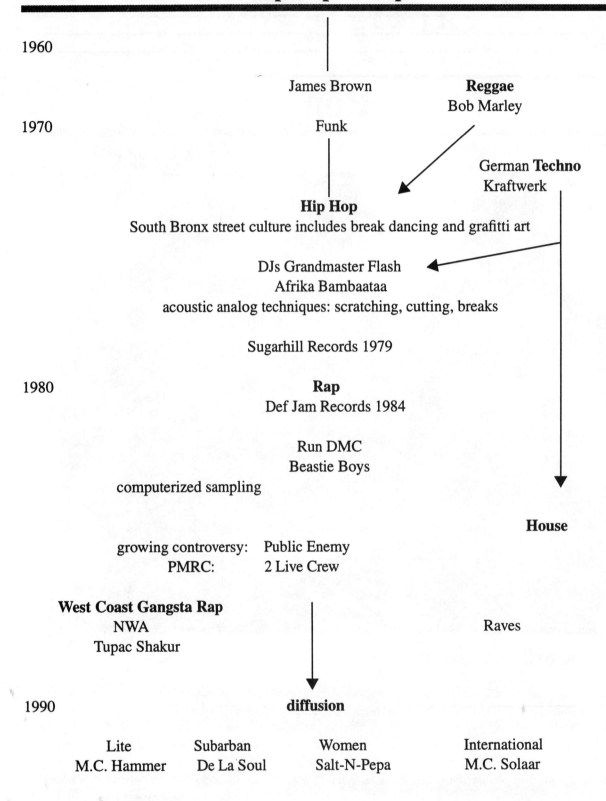

1960

James Brown   **Reggae**
Bob Marley

1970   Funk

German **Techno**
Kraftwerk

Hip Hop
South Bronx street culture includes break dancing and grafitti art

DJs Grandmaster Flash
Afrika Bambaataa
acoustic analog techniques: scratching, cutting, breaks

Sugarhill Records 1979

1980   **Rap**
Def Jam Records 1984

Run DMC
Beastie Boys

computerized sampling

House

growing controversy: Public Enemy
PMRC: 2 Live Crew

West Coast Gangsta Rap   Raves
NWA
Tupac Shakur

1990   **diffusion**

Lite   Subarban   Women   International
M.C. Hammer   De La Soul   Salt-N-Pepa   M.C. Solaar

Reggae: Prelude to Rap

I. Early Styles leading up to Reggae

    1.   **Ska** 1960: combination of indigenous Mento with R&B
- emphasized off beat rhythms
- brass influenced by Mexican Mariachi
- R&B sax solos
- Skatalites important group

    2.   Rock Steady 1965: slower tempo, more rhythmic
- toasting (later called Dubbing) introduced more active bass

    3.   Poppa-Top: more rhythmic version of Rock Steady
- Desmond Dekker: *Israelites* 1969

II. Reggae (literally Kings Music) main period 1969-1976

    1.   reflection of Rastafarian religion:
- started in 1930s worshiping Ethiopian Emperor Haile Selassie as prophet
- dreadlocks and marijuana

    2.   musical characteristics built on Ska and Rock Steady:
- slow, loping tempo
- emphasis on syncopated bass line
- use of keyboards, esp, organ
- off beat rhythm guitar

III. Important Groups

    1.   Mayals, 1968 recording: *Do The Reggey*

    2.   1973 documentary film by Perry Hengell: *Harder They Come*, starring Jimmy Cliff, helped Reggae's popularity in US

    3.   **Bob Marley** (1945-1981) **and the Wailers** (Peter Tosh and Bunny Livingstone) became Reggae's most popular band
- album: *Burnin'* with hit single *I Shot The Sheriff* 1973

Hip Hop

I. Origins: DJs in South Bronx and Harlem, influenced by Jamaican Toasting, began to speak (rap) over short samples of records, usually from the funk tradition.

    1.   important DJs:
- Kool DJ Herc. (Clive Cambell) began sampling in 1973
- Afrika Bambaataa: created Zulu Nation, techno influenced by Kraftwerk
- **Grandmaster Flash** (Joseph Saddler) became most popular DJ in 1976

    2.   early techniques:
- scratching
- variable speed control
- adding reverb and echo
- quickly alternating between two turntables (cutting)

    3.   two diverse outside influences:
- Jamaican Reggae
- European synthesizer bands, especially Kraftwerk

4. Gil Scott Heron: combined jazz and poetry
5. 1979: **Sugarhill Records** founded by Slyvia Robinson
   - *Rappers Delight*, first rap record to crack top 40
   - Grandmaster Flash created social statements:
     • *Freedom* 1979
     • *The Message* 1982
6. two parallel arts:
   - break dancing
   - graffiti art

Jean-Michel Basquiat

Beginning as the obscure graffiti artist SAMO, Jean-Michel Basquiat (1960-1988) became a protege of Andy Warhol, emerging as one of the most celebrated artists of the 1980s. He led a self-destructive, tumultuous life, similar to that of Jimi Hendrix, dying of a heroin overdose at age 27. His work was influenced by Hip-Hop and jazz. *Basquiat*, a film by painter Julian Schnabel with a cast including David Bowie and Courtney Love, was released in 1995.

Rap

Essentially consisting of spoken lyrics recited over active funk-derived rhythms, comprehensibility of the words is of prime important in rap. Two styles developed: on the East Coast, the lyrics tended toward a denunciation of racism, while the West Coast emphasized gangs and police violence.

I. **East Coast Rap:** social and political focus of Def Jam Record Company formed in 1984 by Russell Simmons and Rick Rubin (recorded Run-DMC and Beastie Boys).

1. **Run-DMC:** formed in 1982 by DJ Jason Mizel and rappers Darryl-McDaniels and Joseph Run Simmons
   - first three albums:
     • *Run DMC* 1984 (originally 12' single) first gold rap album, used Latino guitarist, Eddie Martinez
     • *King of Rock* with Tony Torrez and the Latin Rascals
     • *Raising Hell* 1986, collaboration with Aerosmith (*Walk This Way*) created crossover audience, sold over 3 million
2. **Public Enemy** featuring Chuck D (Carlton Ridenhour) sometimes called The Black Panthers Of Rap
   - Strong political messages contained in 1990 album: *It Takes A Nation Of Millions To Hold Us Back* sold 1 million, *Fight The Power* Spike Lee Video samples James Brown
   - sped up the tempo and used complex textures of sampling and noise
   - criticized for anti-semitic statements
3. **2 Live Crew** criticized for foul and violent language and misogynistic statements:
   - unsuccessfully tried for obscenity in Florida
   - 1989 album: *As Nasty As They Wanna Be* banned in some states
   - next album *Banned in U.S.A.* 1990 capitalized on controversy added guitar solos
4. **Beastie Boys**, rock oriented White rap group. First rap group to have albums that went gold, platinum, and double platinum: *License To Ill*

II. West Coast Gangsta Rap: emphasized gangs, criticized for promoting violence

  1. **N.W.A.** (Niggas With Attitude) rapped of gangs and Police Violence
      - second album: *Straight Outta Compton* 1988 sold million copies

N.W.A. © CORBIS

  2. Ice Cube (Oshea Jackson) formerly with N.W.A.
  3. Ice-T (Tracy Marrow) recorded controversial *Cop Killer* from 1992 album *Body Count* which Warner Bros. deleted after first issue

III. Female Rappers:

  1. Salt-N-Pepa, first female hip hop group, updated girl group tended towards a lighter, non-political approach,
  2. Sister Souljah (Lisa Williamson) criticism by Presidential candidate Bill Clinton turned her into a national figure.
  3. Queen Latifah emphasized an Afro centric sense of pride

IV. Other Rappers:

  1. Arrested Development: Southern Rap
  2. De La Soul: Suburban Rap
  3. Hammer (formerly M.C. Hammer) Lite Rap
  4. M.C. Solaar: Senegelese rapper records in Paris

V. During the 1990s many rappers abandoned gangsta rap in favor of a more positive approach focusing on community involvement:

1. The Jungle Bros. 1990 Politics of Nature tour included talks on creating an African American consciousness
2. KRS-One (Knowledge Reigns Supreme Over Nearly Everyone) organized Stop The Violence which contributed $500,000 to the National Urban League
3. KTRS-One, with Run DMC and Queen Latifah formed H.E.A.L. Yourself
4. M.C. Hammer worked with inner city kids of Oakland
5. X-Clan organized voter registration and anti-crack seminars
6. Female rapper Yo-Yo started Intelligent Black Women's Coalition

Addenda: African American Poverty in the 1980s

1980: 31% of African Americans lived in poverty, three times that of Whites
1987: 34% of African American teenagers were unemployed. compared to 17% of Whites;
by 1992 teen unemployment had risen to 40%
1989: 1600 teen homicides
1992: 59% of African American families were female headed, compared to 24% in 1964
1992: homicide becomes the leading cause of death for teens

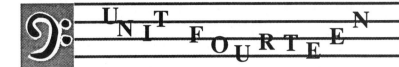

MTV and 80s Superstars

Michael Jackson, 1995. AGENCE FRANCE PRESSE/CORBIS-BETTMANN.

MTV

During the early 1980s. MTV (Music Television) replaced radio as the most important disseminator of rock, making its formation one of the decisive events in the music's brief history and continuing White Corporate America's appropriation of popular music. While praised for its visual creativity, MTV has been criticized for substituting glitz and visual effects for musical substance.

I. Techo-America: growth of electronic industry 1980s

    1.   by 1989, 98.2% of American households had TV, 85% color
        -    average High School student watched 3-4 hrs of TV/day, and by graduation will have spent more time watching TV than sitting in classrooms

    2.   1989: 97 million VCRs

    3.   video games: Atari grossed 1.3 billion in home videos 1983

II. Birth of MTV

    1.   August 1, 1981: aided by the growth of cable following deregulation, Warner Communications and American Express invested $20 million to start MTV
        -    marketed under 25 generation, used sophisticated marketing strategies
        -    featured non-stop 3-min selections 24 hours a day
        -    initially featured only White, mostly British (because of their greater experience with visuals)

    2.   White, mid-west audience first targeted

    3.   growth:

	1981	1983	1989
	2.5 million viewers	17 million	46 million
	300 stations	2000	5000

    4.   MTV's success impacted on all phases of the music industry:
        -    videos became mandatory
        -    major labels tours synchronized tours with video releases

    5.   creative outlet for film makers using techniques from French New Wave, Sci.Fi.:
        -    lap dissolves, multiple imaging, surrealism

III. MTV and Electro Pop: MTV synthesizer-dominated bands swept US 1983

    1.   Duran Duran, British band neo-romantics, first to achieve fame from MTV exposure
    2.   Bon Jovi, Eurythmics, Talking Heads, Devo among other early bands on MTV
    3.   David Bowie's career rejuvenated
    4.   **Michael Jackson**

MTV Superstars of the 1980s

Most of the following owe their superstar status to MTV, with Michael Jackson, Prince and Madonna disseminating a dance music influenced by funk and disco.

I. Michael Jackson (1958-) dancer-vocalist, became most important rock star of the 1980s

    1.   grew up in Gary, Indiana, performing with family ensemble (Tito, Jermaine, Jackie, and Marlon) under the direction of father, Joe Jackson
    2.   with Motown 1968-1976 as Jackson 5
    3.   1976 signed with Epic as The Jacksons
    4.   solo career: highlighted with Quincy Jones collaborations:
        •   *Off The Wall* 1979
    5.   *Thriller* 1982 blockbuster collaboration with Quincy Jones:
        -    sold over 40 million, #1 album for 37 weeks, stayed on the charts for 65 weeks
        -    7 top ten singles
        -    12 Grammys
        -    video, "The Making of Michael Jackson's Thriller", sold 1/2 million (third behind Jane Fonda's Workout and Raiders of the Lost Ark)

- smooth, crisp mix of styles:
  - *Wanna Be*: Dance-funk, *The Girl Is Mine* - pop ballad (with Paul McCartney), *Beat It*: hard rock (with Eddie Van Halen), *Billie Jean*: disco

5. After protest by Columbia Records, *Billie Jean* appears on MTV 1982, breaking MTV all-White policy

II. Prince (Rogers Nelson 1959-): created a pop synthesis of disco, funk, and new wave

1. grew up in Minneapolis and began producing records 1977
2. influenced by ad-man Chris Moon, began using explicit sexuality
3. Signed with Warner Bros. 1978:
   Dirty Mind 1980 criticized for explicit sexual references
4. 1984: film/sound track **Purple Rain**
5. 1985 formed Paisley Park Record Co.

III. Madonna (Madonna Louise Ciccone 1958-): with her dance-oriented pop-rock plus punk persona, became the most successful female rock performer of the 1980s.

1. grew up in Detroit and attended Univ. of Michigan as dance major
2. briefly with Alvin Ailey before moving to Paris 1979 to perform with Disco review
3. started musical career and released first record in 1983 emphasizing sexually suggestive disco style
4. 1984: controversial *Like A Virgin* appears on MTV initiates (PMRC) Parents Music Resource Center
5. Film career:
   - *Desperately Seeking Susan* 1985
   - documentary: *Truth or Dare* 1991

The Boss

I. Bruce Springsteen (1949-) growing out of the singer-songwriters of the 1970s, Springsteen's career peaked in the 1980s when he became associated with blue-collar, middle class. His style evolved from a Dylanesque folk to a more mainstream rock.

1. son of a bus driver, grew up in Freehold, New Jersey, began playing guitar at age 13
2. after long apprenticeship discovered by John Hammond and signed with Columbia, first release: *Greetings From Asbury Park*, unsuccessful
3. 1974 formed E-Street band and moved towards harder rock style
4. important review in *Rolling Stone* by Jon Landau launched career
5. 1975: *Born To Run*, appears on covers of *Time* and *Newsweek*
6. important albums of the 1980s:
   - *The River* 1980
   - *Nebraska* 1982
   - **Born in the USA** 1984, contained 5 hit singles and sold over 11 million
   - In recent years Springsteen has become increasingly involved in charity concerts and philanthropic ventures (donating $200,000 to Amnesty International)

Bruce Springsteen © Lynn Goldsmith/CORBIS

Other Bands That Emerged During the 1980s

Other bands that blended funk, alternative and new wave into a commercially success includes the following:

I. **U2:** Paul Hewson (Bono), The Edge (David Evans), Adam Clayton, Larry Mullen, Jr. from Dublin, Ireland, features ensemble over solos

    1.   1980 first release: *Boy*

    2.   political causes important: 1982: *Sunny Bloody Sunday* performed in Belfast

    -    important albums:

        •   *War* 1983

        •   *Joshua Tree* 1987 in support of Amnesty International

    3.   1984 Brian Eno began producing: New Wave style

        •   *The Unforgettable Fire* 1984

        •   *Rattle and Hum* 1988

II. **Red-Hot-Chili Peppers:** neo-funk influenced by Stevie Wonder

III. **Neo Traditional Singer Songwriters** intensified earlier acoustic style

    1. John Cougar Mellencamp (1951-) one of the main supporters of the Farm Aid benefits
       - breakthrough album *American Fool* 1982
    2. Tracy Chapman (1964-) revived the spirit of 60's protest folk-rock
    3. Tom Petty (1953-) influenced by Dylan and Southern Rock

World Music

The 1980s saw an increase in the interaction of traditional world music and pop.

I. Influence from Africa

    1. Juju: Nigerian mix of Rock with African
       - Sunny Ade
    2. Youssou N' Dour from Senegal
    3. Ladysmith Black Mambuzo: South African Gospel choir

II. India

    1. Sitarist Ravi Shankar's influence goes back to the Psychedelic 60s
       - *West Meets East* 1966 collaboration with Yehudi Menuhin
       - performance at 1967 Monterey Pop
       - influence on George Harrison and the Beatles

Western Musicians Incorporating World Music

III. **Paul Simon** (1942-): evolving career after 1970.

    1. Gospel: *Loves Me Like A Rock* 1973 (with the Dixie Hummingbirds)
    2. Country-Funk: *One Trick Pony* 1980 (film soundtrack)
    3. World Music: *Graceland* 1986: eclectic album employed South African groups, Cajun, and Country sounds with Linda Ronstadt, Youssou N'Dour (criticized for working in apartheid South Africa); *Rhythm of the Saints* 1990: uses Afro-Brazilian percussion
    4. *The Capeman* 1998 Broadway musical

IV. **Peter Gabriel,** formerly with Genesis

    • *So* 1986

V. **David Byrne,** formerly with the Talking Heads

VI. **Billy Hart,** drummer of Grateful Dead long interested in various World Music percussion

Addenda 1: Benefits

During the 1980s a renewal of the 1960s use of music for social betterment resulted in a number of benefit events. These events often were televised throughout the world live through world-wide satellite technology:

1. *1984: Ethiopian Benefit Concert in Albert Hall, England*
2. *1985: Live Aid combined simultaneous concerts in London and Philadelphia*
3. *1985: Willie Nelson organizes the first of the Farm Aid benefit concerts*
4. *We Are The World, organized by Quincy Jones*

Addenda 2: PMRC Censorship in the 1980s

1. *Parents Music Resource Center founded in Washington D.C. 1985*
    committee of 20 included 17 wives of prominent politicians including Tipper Gore and Susan Baker (wife of Sec. of State), also ties to Christian Right (Madonna's "Like A Virgin" said to be the catalyst that started PMRC)
2. *Public Hearing held Sept. 1985 (reminiscent of Payola Hearings)*
    -   *PMRC cited concern over 5 issues:*
        1) drugs 2) suicide 3) violence 4) occult 5) sex (not racial bigotry)
    -   *suggested parental warning labels: X explicit lyrics, V violence, O occult*
    -   *opposing PMRC was Zappa et al citing First Amendment Rights*
        Zappa suggested hearing a covert attempt to boost country sales
        compromise solution: generic label "Parental Advisory/Explicit Lyrics"
3. *1988 PMRC released video "Rising to the Challenge" criticized metal and rap*
4. *reactions to PMRC:*
    Wal-Mart, Sears, JC Penney refused to sell stickered albums
    1990: 13 States held hearings on regulating record stores
    1992 Omaha: four record outlets which sold stickered albums were charged with violating Nebraska's Harmful to Minor's Law

Media Sensationalism/Important Civil Cases

1. *1985: Ozzy Osbourne sued by parents of California teenager who committed suicide after hearing "Suicide Solution"- thrown out of court*
2. *1988: Owner of record store fined for selling 2 Live Crew's "Move Something" to police informer*
3. *1989: NWA's "Fuck the Police" caused boycott of Warner Bros*
4. *1990: 2 Live Crew's "Nasty As They Wanna Be" became first recording legally declared obscene in a federal district court- overturned in 1993*
    obscenity: 1) lacks serious....value 2) appeals to prurient interests 3) offensive to community standards
5. *1990: two teens were found dead clutching lyrics of Metallica's "Fade to Black" 20/20 TV expose*
6. *Judas Priest's subliminal messages on "Stained Glass" said to cause two Nevada teens to kill themselves with a shotgun - cleared of all charges after claimants found mentally incompetent*
7. *Madonna's "Justify My Love" became first video banned on MTV*
8. *Dead Kennedy's sued by parent on obscenity charges: Jello Biafra arrested for distributing harmful material to a minor - ended in favor of Biafra*
9. *1992: Sister Souljah music reflecting Rodney King incident was attacked by Pres. Clinton*
10. *1992: Ice Tea's "Cop Killer" drew wrath of George Bush, Dan Quayle, Oliver North, Charlton Heston and Beverley Sills (not backed by National Black Police Association)*
11. *Three rappers involved in highly reported violent crimes: Snoop Doggy Dog and Tupac Shakur arrested for aggravated assault and Flavor Flav (Of Public Enemy) for attempted murder*
12. *Murders of Notorious B.I.G. and Tupac Shakur*

Alternative Music for Generation X

Kurt Cobain © S.I.N./CORBIS

More a philosophy than a musical style, alternative music, like 50s Rock and Roll and Punk reflected a dissatisfaction with commercial, mainstream music, and created new sounds by twisting and contorting earlier styles, techniques sometimes referred to as "Post Modernism". New dress styles and dance forms (moshing and stage diving) also exemplified the predominating attitude of purposelessness and nihilism. Beginning like Punk, as an underground movement, Alternative, led by Nirvana, had by the mid 1990s, become America's most popular musical genre, selling over 110 million records in 1996.

Alternative vs. Mainstream

While much variety exist within Alternative, some of the common points of agreement are illustrated in the following comparison with mainstream music:

alternative	mainstream
twist, contorts, juxtaposes conventions,	conventional
modern up to date	often referring to older styles.
often eclectic mix of styles	united in single style
raw, unvarnished	processed, glitzy, synthetic
often murky, cloudy, layered recording	clear, slick mix
anti singing	singing
words often brutal, confrontational	lyrics safe, status quo
sophisticated, abstract lyrics	simple, easy to grasp
negative	neutral or positive
no difference between performers and audience	social stars distanced from audience
clothing same as audience	glitz clothes
designed for small, specific demographic audience (fanbase)	aimed at large, universal audience
	promoted through indies, fanzines, college radio MTV, major labels
touring small venues	large stadium, satellite hookups
gender not emphasized	gender distinction important (sexy)

Historical Influences

I. Velvet Underground

    Big Star 1970s underground Memphis band with Alex Chilton

II. Punk, especially Sex Pistols

III. Immediate Precursors (Post Punk):

    1.   California Hardcore Punk: Black Flag, X, The Minutemen, The Dead Kennedys
    2.   Athens, Georgia early 1980s: R.E.M., B 52s
    3.   Minneapolis bands mid 1980s:
        -   Hüsker Dü
        -   The Replacements, led by Paul Westerberg

Sonic Youth:

New York postmodern guitar noise band influenced by the beats and Sci-Fi cyberpunk writer Philip K. Dick (1928-1982). Had direct impact on Nirvana. Kim Gordon, bass and vocals, Lee Rinaldo, Thurston Moore, guitar, Steve Shelley, drums

    -   dense textures and avant garde noise
    -   unusual guitar tunings and techniques
    -   albums from the 1980s:
        • *Sonic Youth* 1982

- *Confusion Is Sex* 1983
- *Kill Yr. Idols*
- *Sonic Death*
- *Bad Moon Rising* 1985
- *Death Valley '69*
- *EVOL* 1986
- *Sister* 1987
- *Master-Dik*
- **Daydream Nation 1988**

R.E.M. © Moshe Shai/CORBIS

R.E.M.:

Michael Stipe, vocals, Peter Buck, guitar, Mike Mills, bass, Bill Berry, drums, became first alternative band to establish pop success with idiosyncratic blend of punk, new wave and folk-rock

- formed in Athens, GA 1980, first hit single, *Radio Free Europe* 1981
- later albums include: *Murmur* 1983, *Reckoning* 1984, *Document* 1987
- *Green* 1988, first album with Warner Bros. including *Orange Crush* and lyrical *South Central Rain*
- 1988 voted best "America's best rock & Roll Band" by Rolling Stone
- *Out of Time* 1991 including *Losing My Religion*
- *Automatic For The People* 1992

Seattle Grunge

Following Athens and Minneapolis, Seattle, with its music known as Grunge, became the most publicized alternative scene of the late 1980s. The Grunge look, influenced by Punk, included ripped plaid lumberjack shirts and Doc Marten boots. The uniqueness of the area was captured in TV programs *Twin Peaks*, *Northern Exposure*, and in the film, *Singles*. By 1993, Seattle grunge was dominating the charts.

I. **Sub Pop:** Subterranean Pop Recording Co. formed 1986 by Bruce Pavitt and Jonathan Poneman, starting as a fanzine, became the leading promoter and distributor of Seattle-based bands, originally making limited pressings before selling to major labels.

II. **Nirvana:** formed in 1987 with **Kurt Cobain** (1967-1994) achieved MTV blockbuster album with *Nevermind* 1991 (including smash hit *Smells Like Teen Spirit*) sold from Sub Pop to Geffen

- combined punk/pop metal with Beatles' lyricism and hooks
- featured alternating loud/soft sections
- Cobain committed suicide in April, 1994

III. **Other Grunge Bands** an estimated 1000 bands were (are) active in the area. Some of the most important include:

1. Soundgarden: metal-influenced, first recorded in 1987 *Screaming Life*, first Seattle band to sign with major label
2. Pearl Jam: featuring vocalist Eddie Vedder, rivaled Nirvana in popularity
   - first album *Ten* released in 1991
3. Mudhoney formed by Mark Arm and Steve Turner
4. Afghan Whigs
5. Hole: led by Courtney Love, widow of Kurt Cobain
6. Alice in Chains

Alternative Categories in the 1990s

The following reflect some of the myriad categories of alternative:

I. **Grebo** (British version of Grunge)
1. Mega City Four
2. Ned's Atomic Dustbin

II. **Dream Pop** (or Shoegazers) (or Miasma) blurred, dense layers obscuring melody predominantly British Bands:
1. My Bloody Valentine
2. Catherine Wheel

III. **Feedback**: similar to Dream Pop but more intense use of distortion, feedback, and white noise:
- Jesus And Mary Chain, most important
  - *Psychocandy* influential 1985 release

IV. Art Rock Alternative: influenced by New Wave and 60s Psychedelia, arty names and album covers:

1. Cocteau Twins, Scottish trio featuring vocalist Elizabeth Fraser singing unique, invented language:
    - *Blue Bell Knoll* 1988
2. Dead Can Dance: combines Celtic with Middle East
3. Cabaret Voltaire

V. American Guitar Bands influenced by the Stooges:

1. Dinosaur Jr.
2. Sonic Youth

VI. British Guitar Bands

1. The Smiths, led by vocalist Morrissey
2. The Fall
3. Kitchens Of Distinction

VII. Gothic (or Death) focuses on apocalyptic morbidity

1. Bauhaus
2. Sisters Of Mercy

VIII. Rave and **Techno**

IX. Industrial originated in American Midwest: dark, desperate sounds of sample-heavy keyboard and metal guitar, concerts scenes of violent moshing.

1. Ministry, from Chicago. began as techo-pop with *Sympathy* 1983, evolved to Industrial by 1988 with *The Mind Is A Terrible Thing To Taste*
2. Nine Inch Nails, from Cleveland
3. Throbbing Gristle

X. Jazz Influenced

1. Dave Matthews Band
2. Phish (Trey Anastasia, guitar, Page McConell, keyboards, Mike Gordon, bass, Jan Fishman, percussion) have been compared to the Grateful Dead with their eclectic mix of styles and loyal fanbase.

Prominent Women Singer-Songwriters of the 1990s

Alternative music is reflected in the growing prominence of women, which culminated in the all-women **Lilith Fair** concert tour beginning a three year run in 1997 which set all-time box office records for Rock concert tours. Some of these singer-songwriters, all of whose music contains social commentary, include:

1. Suzanne Vega (1959-) intense folk-based style
    - breakthrough albums include:
        - *Luka* 1987
        - *Tom's Diner* 1990
2. Tori Amos (1963-) uses classical piano in complex and politically charged songs

- founder of RAINN (Rape Abuse and Incest National Network)
- first recording *Little Earthquakes* 1992
3. Bjork (b. 1965 Reykjavic, Iceland)
   - whimsical eclectic mix of punk, techno and jazz
   - solo album *Debut* 1993 international hit
4. Sinead O'Connor (b. 1966 Dublin, Ireland) mixes Celtic and Hip-Hop with lyrics championing Women's and Children's rights hit single *Nothing Compares To You* 1990
5. Sarah McLachlan (b. 1969 Halifax, Nova Scotia) moody evocative folk-pop organized Lilith Fair
   - breakthrough album *Fumbling Towards Ecstasy* 1993
6. Indigo Girls, formed in 1985 by Amy Ray and Emily Sailers, updated folk style with sophisticated lyrics incorporating mythological and classical themes with social causes, especially Women's, Gay and Lesbian rights, environmental concerns, and gun control
   - characteristic recording *Swamp Ophelia* 1994

Listening Suggestions

The following is a list of recordings played during a recent class at the University of Nebraska taught by Tom Larson.

One: Black Roots

1. R&B Box Set Vol 1: Five Guys Named Moe—Louis Jordan
2. Blues cassette tape: some tunes by Muddy Waters, Bo Diddley, Willie Dixon, etc.
3. Chess R&R Vol 1: Rocket 88—Jackie Brenston 1951
4. Rock Music Collection cassette: Blueberry Hill—Fats Domino
5. Little Richards Greatest Songs: Lucille
6. Little Richards Greatest Songs: Tutti Frutti 1955
7. Little Richards Greatest Songs: Long Tall Sally
8. Little Richards Greatest Songs: Good Golly Miss Molly
9. Chess R&R Vol 1: Bo Diddley—Bo Diddley
10. Chess R&R Vol 2: Who Do You Love—Bo Diddley
11. The Mighty Bo Diddley: Ain't It Good To Be Free
12. The Mighty Bo Diddley: BD Put The Rock In R&R
13. Hand Jive—Eric Clapton
14. Great Twenty Eight: Maybellene— Chuck Berry 1955
15. Great Twenty Eight.: Johnny B Goode—Chuck Berry
16. Great Twenty Eight: School Days—Chuck Berry
17. Great Twenty Eight: Roll Over Beethoven—Chuck Berry
18. Great Twenty Eight: Nadine—Chuck Berry
19. Ray Charles Vol 1: Jumpin' In The Mornin'
20. Ray Charles Vol l: The Sun's Gonna Shine Again
21. Ray Charles Vol 2: I Got A Woman
22. Ray Charles Vol 3: What'd I Say
23. Ray Charles Vol 3: I'm Movin' On 1953
24. Best Of: You Send Me—Sam Cooke
25. Best Of: For Sentimental Reasons—Sam Cooke
26. Doo Wop cassette: Cab Driver—Mills Brothers
27. Doo Wop cassette: Old Man River—Ravens
28. Doo Wop cassette: Cryin' In the Chapel—Orioles
29. Doo Wop cassette: Sh-Boom—Chords
30. Doo Wop cassette: Earth Angel—Penguins
31. Doo Wop cassette: Get A Job—Silhouettes
32. Doo Wop cassette: Book of Love—Monotones
33. Doo Wop cassette: Smoke Gets In Your Eyes—Platters
34. Doo Wop cassette: Young Blood—Coasters
35. Doo Wop cassette: Spanish Harlem, On Broadway—Drifters

Two: White Roots

36. Woody Guthrie cassette: Pretty Boy Floyd—Guthrie
37. Dylan's Greatest Hits: Times They Are A Changin' —Dylan
38. Country Music Sampler cassette: I Truly Understand, You Love Another Man—Rourke Family Band
39. Country Music Sampler cassette: Why Do You Wander—Bill Monroe
40. Country Music Sampler cassette: Blue Ridge Cabin Home—Flatt & Skruggs

41. Country Music Sampler cassette: San Antonio Rose, Steel Guitar Rag—Bob Wills
42. Country Music Sampler cassette: Hey Good Lookin', Cold, Cold Heart, Jambalaya, Your Cheatin' Heart —Hank Williams

Three: White Rock & Roll

43. Bill Haley's Greatest Hits: Rock Around The Clock
44. Bill Haley's Greatest Hits: See You Later, Alligator
45. Bill Haley's Greatest Hits: Shake, Rattle & Roll
46. Atlantic Soul Classics: Shake, Rattle & Roll—Joe Turner
47. Elvis Complete Masters, Vol 1: My Happiness
48. Elvis Complete Masters, Vol 1: That's All Right Mama 1954
49. Elvis Complete Masters, Vol 1: Blue Moon of Kentucky
50. Elvis Complete Masters, Vol 1: Mystery Train
51. Elvis Complete Masters, Vol 1: Heartbreak Hotel
52. Elvis Complete Masters, Vol 2: Don't Be Cruel
53. Elvis Complete Masters, Vol 2: Hound Dog
54. Buddy Holly Original Master Tapes: Rock Around With Ollie Vee
55. Buddy Holly Original Master Tapes: That'll Be The Day 1956
56. Buddy Holly Original Master Tapes: Peggy Sue
57. Buddy Holly Original Master Tapes: Not Fade Away
58. Buddy Holly Original Master Tapes: Oh Boy
59. Buddy Holly Original Master Tapes: Words Of Love
60. Buddy Holly Original Master Tapes: Everyday
61. Buddy Holly Original Master Tapes: Well All Right
62. Buddy Holly Original Master Tapes: It Doesn't Matter Anymore
63. Buddy Holly Original Master Tapes: True Love Ways
64. Not Fade Away: Peggy Sue Got Married
65. Not Fade Away: Not Fade Away
66. Original Sun Greatest Hits: Whole Lotta Shakin'—JL Lewis
67. Original Sun Greatest Hits: Great Balls of Fire—JL Lewis
68. Rock Misc Collection cassette: Blue Suede Shoes—Carl Perkins
69. All Time Greatest Hits: Bye Bye Love—Everly Brothers
70. All Time Greatest Hits: Wake Up, Little Susie—Everly Brothers
71. All Time Greatest Hits: All I Have To Do Is Dream—Everly Brothers
72. All Time Greatest Hits: Cathy's Clown—Everly Brothers

Four: Pop Rock

73. Best Of Frankie Avalon: Venus
74. Billboard Top Hits 1961: Moody River—Pat Boone
75. Girl Groups cassette: Will You Still Love Me—Shirelles 1960
76. Girl Groups cassette: Da Doo Ron Ron—Crystals
77. Girl Groups cassette: Be My Baby—Ronny & the Ronettes
78. Girl Groups cassette: Leader of the Pack—Shangri-Las
79. CDISC Belkin 138: River Deep, Mountain High—Ike & Tina Turner
80. Best of Dick Dale: Let's Go Trippin'
81. Pipeline/Doors/Dead Kennedys cassette: Pipeline—Chantays 1963
82. Best of Dick Dale: Hava Nagila
83. Best of Dick Dale: Riders In The Sky

84. Louie, Louie—Kingsmen
85. Rock Misc Collection cassette: Wipe Out—Surfaris 1963
86. Four Freshmen cassette: Shar-Me 1955
87. Four Freshmen cassette: Day By Day
88. Beach Boys Greatest Hits: Surfin' Safari 1962
89. Beach Boys Greatest Hits: Little Duece Coupe
90. Beach Boys Greatest Hits: I Get Around 1964
91. Beach Boys Greatest Hits: Surfer Girl 1963
92. Beach Boys Greatest Hits: Fun Fun Fun
93. Pet Sounds: God Only Knows 1966
94. Pet Sounds: Don't Talk 1966
95. Pet Sounds: Caroline, No 1966
96. Pet Sounds: I Know There's An Answer 1966
97. Pet Sounds: I'm Waiting For The Day 1966
98. Pet Sounds: Wouldn't It Be Nice 1966
99. Beach Boys Greatest Hits: Good Vibrations 1966

Five: Soul

100. Motown Legends: I Second That Emotion—SR & The Miracles
101. Chicago/Blues Sampler/Motown cassette: Mickeys Monkey—Miracles
102. Chicago/Blues Sampler/Motown cassette: The One Who Really Loves You—Mary Wells
103. Chicago/Blues Sampler/Motown cassette: Quicksand—Martha & The Vandellas
104. Chicago/Blues Sampler/Motown cassette: Pride & Joy—Marvin Gaye 1964
105. Chicago/Blues Sampler/Motown cassette: Shotgun—Jr Walker 1965
106. Chicago/Blues Sampler/Motown cassette: I Can't Help Myself—Four Tops
107. Chicago/Blues Sampler/Motown cassette: Aint Too Proud To Beg—Tempts 1964
108. Chicago/Blues Sampler/Motown cassette: Stop In The Name of Love—Supremes 1965
109. Chicago/Blues Sampler/Motown cassette: I Heard It Through The Grapevine—Gladys Knight 1968
110. Motown Legends: Uptight—Stevie Wonder
111. Atlantic Soul Classics: Green Onions—Booker T & The MG's 1962
112. Atlantic Soul Classics: In The Midnight Hour—Wilson Pickett 1965
113. Atlantic Soul Classics: Soul Man -Sam & Dave 1967
114. Atlantic Soul Classics: I've Been Loving You Too Long—Otis Redding
115. Mr Big Stuff: Mr Big Stuff—Jean Knight 1970
116. Mr Big Stuff: Don't Talk About Jody—Jean Knight 1970
117. Atlantic Soul Classics: When A Man Loves A Woman—Percy Sledge 1966
118. Aretha Franklin 30 Greatest Hits: Respect
119. Aretha Franklin 30 Greatest Hits: Natural Woman 1967
120. Aretha Franklin 30 Greatest Hits: Eleanor Rigby 1969
121. Aretha Franklin 30 Greatest Hits: Bridge Over Troubled Water 1971
122. R&B Box Set Vol 4: For Your Precious Love—Jerry Butler
123. O'Jays Greatest Hits: For The Love Of Money 1972
124. James Brown, Star Time: Please Please Me 1956
125. James Brown, Star Time: Try Me 1958
126. Live At The Apollo: Introduction
127. Live At The Apollo: Please Please Me
128. James Brown, Star Time: Night Train 1962
129. James Brown, Star Time: Out Of Sight
130. James Brown, Star Time: Papa's Got A Brand New Bag 1965
131. James Brown, Star Time: I Feel Good 1965

132. James Brown, Star Time: Cold Sweat 1967
133. James Brown, Star Time: Say It Loud
134. James Brown, Star Time: Mother Popcorn 1969
135. James Brown, Star Time: Get Up, Sex Machine 1970
136. James Brown, Star Time: Get Up, Get Into It, Get Involved
137. James Brown, Star Time: There It Is 1972
138. James Brown, Star Time: Funky President 1974
139. James Brown, Star Time: I Got A Bag Of My Own
140. James Brown, Star Time: Unity. Pt 1 1984

Six: Poetic Interlude

141. Dylan's Greatest Hits: Subterranean Homesick Blues
142. Bob Dylan Gaslight Cafe cassette: Barbara Allen
143. Dylan's Greatest Hits: Blowin' In The Wind
144. Four Freshmen/Talking JBS Blues cassette: Talking John Birch Society Blues
145. Dylan's Greatest Hits: The Times They Are A Changin'
146. Dylan's Greatest Hits: Like A Rolling Stone
147. Dylan's Greatest Hits: Mr Tambourine Man
148. Dylan's Greatest Hits: Rainy Day Women 1966
149. Nashville Skyline (CDISC 2681): Lay Lady Lay 1969
150. Nashville Skyline (CDISC 2681): Nashville Skyline Rag 1969
151. Tom Dooley cassette: Tom Dooley—Kingston Trio
152. Lenny Bruce Originals: My Trip To Miami—Lenny Bruce
153. Old Friends: Sounds Of Silence—Simon & Garfunkel
154. Old Friends: Sounds Of Silence (w rhythm section)—S&G
155. Old Friends: April Come She Will—S&G
156. Old Friends: Scarborough Fair Canticle—S&G
157. Old Friends 59th Street Bridge Song—S&G
158. Old Friends: Mrs Robinson—S&G
159. Old Friends: The Boxer- S&G
160. Old Friends Bridge Over Troubled Water—S&G Seven: The British Invasion
161. Beatles Live At The BBC: I Got A Woman
162. Beatles Live At The BBC: Youngblood
163. Beatles Live At The BBC: That's All Right Mama
164. Beatles Live At The BBC: Crying, Waiting, Hoping
165. Beatles Live At The BBC: You Really Got A Hold On Me
166. Beatles Live At The BBC: Johnny Be Goode
167. Beatles Live At The BBC: Long Tall Sally
168. Please Please Me: Twist & Shout—Beatles 1963
169. Unsurpassed Masters Vol 1 cassette: Besame Mucho—The Beatles
170. Hard Days Night: Hard Days Night—The Beatles
171. Hard Days Night: And I Love Her—The Beatles
172. Hard Days Night: If I Fell—The Beatles
173. Beatles For Sale: I'll Follow The Sun
174. Beatles For Sale: I'm A Loser
175. Beatles For Sale: Honey Don't
176. Help: You've Got To Hide Your Love Away—The Beatles 1965
177. Help: Yesterday—The Beatles 1965
178. Unsurpassed Masters Vol 2 cassette: We Can Work It Out—The Beatles
179. Rubber Soul: Michelle—The Beatles 1965

180. Revolver: Here, There And Everywhere—The Beatles 1966
181. Revolver: Tomorrow Never Knows—The Beatles 1966
182. Revolver: Eleanor Rigby—The Beatles 1966
183. Revolver: Taxman—The Beatles 1966
184. Revolver: Love You Too—The Beatles 1966
185. Magical Mystery Tour: Strawberry Fields—The Beatles 1967
186. Magical Mystery Tour: Penny Lane—The Beatles 1967
187. Sgt. Peppers: Sgt Peppers—The Beatles 1967
188. Sgt. Peppers: With A Little Help From My Friends—The Beatles 1967
189. Sgt. Peppers: Lucy In The Sky—The Beatles 1967
190. Sgt. Peppers: She's Leaving Home—The Beatles 1967
191. Sgt. Peppers: Being For The Benefit Of Mr Kite—The Beatles 1967
192. Sgt. Peppers: Within You, Without You—The Beatles 1967
193. Sgt. Peppers: When I'm 64—The Beatles 1967
194. Sgt. Peppers: Good Morning, Good Morning—The Beatles 1967
195. Sgt. Peppers: A Day In The Life—The Beatles 1967
196. White Album: Back In The USSR—The Beatles 1968
197. White Album: Happiness Is A Warm Gun—The Beatles 1968
198. White Album: Blackbird—The Beatles 1968
199. White Album: Martha My Dear—The Beatles 1968
200. Abbey Road: Mean Mr Mustard—The Beatles
201. Abbey Road: Polyethylene Pam—The Beatles
202. Abbey Road: She Came In Through The Bathroom Window—The Beatles
203. McCartney: Maybe I'm Amazed—Paul McCartney
204. Plastic Ono Band: Mother—John Lennon
205. Plastic Ono Band: Well, Well, Well—Lennon
206. Plastic Ono Band: Working Class Hero—Lennon
207. Singles Collection, The Rolling Stones (cut 1/1): Come On
208. Singles Collection, The Rolling Stones (cut 1/2): I Wanna Be Loved
209. Singles Collection, The Rolling Stones (cut 1/3): I Wanna Be Your Man 1963
210. Singles Collection, The Rolling Stones (cut 1/5): Not Fade Away 1964
211. Big Hits, The Rolling Stones (cut 5): It's All Over Now
212. Big Hits, The Rolling Stones (cut 4): Time Is One My Side
213. Singles Collection, The Rolling Stones (cut 1/10): I Just Wanna Make Love
214. Singles Collection, The Rolling Stones (cut 1/19): Satisfaction 1965
215. Singles Collection, The Rolling Stones (cut 2/2): 19th Nervous Breakdown
216. Singles Collection, The Rolling Stones (cut 2/4): Paint It Black
217. Singles Collection, The Rolling Stones (cut 2/12): Ruby Tuesday
218. Singles Collection, The Rolling Stones (cut 2/15): She's A Rainbow
219. Singles Collection, The Rolling Stones (cut 2/11): Let's Spend The Night Together
220. Singles Collection, The Rolling Stones (cut 2/19): Jumpin' Jack Flash 1968
221. Singles Collection, The Rolling Stones (cut 3/1): Street Fighting Man
222. Singles Collection, The Rolling Stones (cut 3/4): Honky Tonk Women
223. Singles Collection, The Rolling Stones (cut 3/7): Brown Sugar
224. Singles Collection, The Rolling Stones (cut 3/8): Wild Horses
225. Exile On Main Street: Rocks Off—The Rolling Stones 1972
226. Exile On Main Street: Sweet Virginia—The Rolling Stones 1972
227. Exile On Main Street: Ventilator Blues—The Rolling Stones 1972
228. Clapton, Who, 70's cassette: My Generation—The Who
229. Tommy: Overture To Tommy—The Who 1969

230. Tommy: Pinball Wizard—The Who 1969
231. Crossroads (CDSIC 2683): Got To Hurry—The Yardbirds
232. Dark Side of the Moon: Opening—Pink Floyd 1973
233. Dark Side of the Moon: Time—Pink Floyd 1973
234. Dark Side of the Moon: Us & Them—Pink Floyd 1973
235. Dark Side of the Moon: Money—Pink Floyd 1973
236. Days Of Future Passed: Lunch Break- Moody Blues
237. Days Of Future Passed: Nights In White Satin—Moody Blues
238. Close To The Edge: Close To The Edge—Yes

Eight: Acid Rock

239. Best Of Jefferson Airplane: Somebody To Love
240. Best Of Jefferson Airplane: White Rabbit
241. Skeletons In The Closet: Casey Jones—Grateful Dead
242. Skeletons In The Closet: Truckin'—Grateful Dead
243. Skeletons In The Closet: The Golden Road—Grateful Dead
244. Skeletons In The Closet: St Stephen—Grateful Dead
245. Skeletons In The Closet: Mexicali Blues—Grateful Dead
246. Skeletons In The Closet: Fried of the Devil—Grateful Dead
247. Santana's Greatest Hits: Oye Como Va
248. Santana's Greatest Hits: Evil Ways
249. Janis Selections: Trouble In Mind—Janis Joplin 1965
250. Sharp CD (cut 1/4): St Louis Blues—Bessie Smith
251. R&B Box Set Vol 2: Hound Dog—Big Mama Thronton
252. Janis Selections: Summertime—Janis Joplin
253. Janis Selections: Try—Janis Joplin 1970
254. Janis Selections: Raise Your Hand—Janis Joplin 1970
255. Janis Selections Move Over- Janis Joplin 1970
256. Janis Selections: Half Moon—Janis Joplin 1970
257. Janis Selections: Mercedes Benz—Janis Joplin 1970
258. Janis Selections: Me And Bobby McGee—Janis Joplin 1970
259. Jimi Hendrix: Hear My Train A Comin'
260. The Ultimate Experience: Hey Joe—Jimi Hendrix 1966
261. The Ultimate Experience: Purple Haze—Jimi Hendrix
262. The Ultimate Experience: The Wind Cries Mary—Jimi Hendrix
263. The Ultimate Experience: Foxy Lady—Jimi Hendrix
264. Jimi Hendrix: Machine Gun II 1969
265. The Ultimate Experience: Star Spangled Banner—Jimi Hendrix 1969
266. The Ultimate Experience: Angel—Jimi Hendrix 1970
267. The Doors: Break On Through
268. The Doors: Light My Fire 1967
269. The Doors: Backdoor Man
270. The Doors: Alabama Song
271. The Doors: The End
272. LA Woman: The Changeling The Doors
273. LA Woman: Been Down So Long—The Doors
274. LA Woman: LA Woman
275. LA Woman: Riders On The Storm—The Doors
276. Ionization—Varese
277. The Song Of The Youth—Stockhausen

278. Freak Out: Hungry Freaks, Daddy—Zappa
279. Freak Out: Who Are The Brain Police—Zappa 1967
280. Freak Out: Go Cry On Somebody Else's Shoulder—Zappa
281. Freak Out: Help I'm A Rock—Zappa
282. Reuben & The Jets: Cheap Thrills—Zappa
283. Reuben & The Jets: Love Of My Life—Zappa
284. Reuben & The Jets: How Could I Be Such A Fool—Zappa
285. Reuben & The Jets: Desiree—Zappa
286. Hot Rats: Peaches En Regalia—Zappa
287. Hot Rats: Willie The Pimp—Zappa
288. Hot Rats: The Gumbo Variation—Zappa
289. Jazz From Hell: Jazz From Hell—Zappa

Nine: Conservative Reaction

290. Original Singles 65-67 Vol I: Mr Tambourine Man—The Byrds
291. Original Singles 65-67 Vol I: Turn, Turn, Turn—The Byrds
292. Original Singles 65-67 Vol I: Eight Miles High—The Byrds
293. Mamas & Papas cassette: California Dreamin'
294. Déjà vu: Carry On—CSN&Y 1970
295. Déjà vu: Teach Your Children—CSN&Y 1970
296. Déjà vu: 4 and 20—CSN&Y 1970
297. Déjà vu: Helpless—CSN&Y 1970
298. Déjà vu: Woodstock—CSN&Y 1970
299. It's So Easy cassette: It's So Easy—Linda Ronstadt
300. Hotel California: Hotel California—The Eagles
301. Rumors: Go Your Own Way—Fleetwood Mac
302. Chronicle: Proud Mary—Creedance Clearwater
303. Chronicle: Bad Moon Rising—Creedance Clearwater
304. Chronicle: Down On The Corner—Creedance Clearwater
305. Best Of The Band: Up On Cripple Creek
306. Best Of The Band: The Weight
307. Best Of The Band: Night They Drove Old Dixie Down
308. Live At The Fillmore East: Statesboro Blues—Allman Bros.
309. Live At The Fillmore East: Hot 'Lanta—Allman Bros.
310. Live At The Fillmore East: Whipping Post—Allman Bros.
311. Second Helping: Swamp Music—Lynyrd Skynyrd
312. Second Helping: Needle & The Spoon—Lynyrd Skynyrd
313. Second Helping: Sweet Home Alabama—Lynyrd Skynyrd 1974
314. ZZ Top cassette:
315. Sweet Baby James: Fire & Rain -James Taylor 1970
316. Hits: Chelsea Morning—Joni Mitchell 1967
317. Hits: Help Me—Joni Mitchell 1974
318. Dry Cleaner From Des Moines—Joni Mitchell
319. Tapestry: I Feel The Earth Move—Carol King 1971
320. Tapestry: Natural Woman—Carol King 1971
321. Van Morrison CDs: Gloria, Moondance, Domino

Ten: Funk & Jazz/Rock

322. Sly Stone CD: I Want To Take You Higher
323. Sly Stone CD: Thank You
324. Sly Stone CD: Everyday People
325. Best Of Parliament: Give Up The Funk—George Clinton
326. Best Of Parliament: Up For The Down Stroke—George Clinton
327. Original Musicquarium: Superstition—Stevie Wonder 1972
328. Original Musicquarium: Living For The City—Stevie Wonder 1973
329. I Am: In The Stone—Earth Wind & Fire
330. Freaky Styley: If You Want Me To Stay—Red Hot Chili Peppers
331. Freaky Styley: The Brothers Cup—Red Hot Chili Peppers
332. Selim—Miles Davis 1970
333. A Long Time Coming: Killing Floor—Electric Flag 1968
334. BS&T cassette: Somethin' Goin On 1968
335. BS&T cassette: Spinning Wheel
336. Chicago: Make Me Smile
337. Jazz CD 3/10: Chameleon—Herbie Hancock 1973
338. JAZZ Web CD 3/12: Birdland—Weather Report 1977
339. Sharp CD 3/6: Romantic Warrior—Return To Forever
340. Jazz CD 3/14: Birds of Fire—Mahavishnu Orchestra

Eleven: Metal

341. Rumble: Rumble—Link Wray 1958
342. Best of Cream: Spoonful 1966
343. Best of Cream: Strange Brew 1967
344. Best of Cream: Sunshine of Your Love 1967
345. Best of Cream: White Room 1968
346. Crossroads: After Midnight 1970—Eric Clapton
347. Crossroads (Layla—Eric Clapton
348. Steppenwolf: Born To Be Wild
349. Aerosrnith's Greatest Hits: Sweet Emotion
350. Led Zeppelin: You Shook Me 1969
351. Led Zeppelin: Dazed & Confused 1969
352. Led Zeppelin: Communication Breakdown 1969
353. Led Zeppelin Box Set Whole Lotta Love
354. Led Zeppelin Box Set: Immigrant Song
355. Led Zeppelin Box Set: Since I've Been Loving You
356. Led Zeppelin Box Set: Black Dog
357. Led Zeppelin Box Set: Goin' To California
358. Led Zeppelin Box Set: Dy'er Maker
359. Led Zeppelin Box Set: Stairway To Heaven
360. Ozzie Osborne cassette: Paranoid
361. Deep Purple Greatest Hits: Hush 1968
362. Hysteria (: Armageddon It—Def Leppard
363. Van Halen II: Dance The Night Away 1979
364. And Justice For All: One—Metallica 1988
365. And Justice For All: The Shortest Straw—Metallica 1988
366. Appetite For Destruction: It's So Easy—Guns N' Roses 1987
367. Rise And Fall Of Ziggy Stardust: Ziggy Stardust—David Bowie 1973

368. Elton John's Greatest Hits: Sorry Seems To Be The Hardest Word
369. Elton John's Greatest Hits: I Guess That's Why They Call It The Blues
370. Double Platinum: Rock & Roll All Night—Kiss 1975
371. A Night At The Opera: Bohemian Rhapsody—Queen 1975

Twelve: Punk

372. Velvet Underground I'm Waiting For The Man 1966
373. Iggy & The Stooges: Search & Destroy 1969
374. New York Dolls: Personality Crisis 1973
375. The Dictators: Cars & Girls 1975
376. Patti Smith: Gloria 1975
377. Richard Hell & The Voidoids: Blank Generation
378. The Ramones: Blitzkrieg Bop 1976
379. Never Mind The Bullocks: God Save The Queen—The Sex Pistols 1977
380. London Calling: London Calling—The Clash 1980
381. Devo: Jocko Homo 1976
382. Elvis Costello: The Angels Wanna Wear My Red Shoes 1977
383. Synchronicity: Synchronicity—The Police 1980

Thirteen: Rap

384. The History 88: I Shot The Sheriff—Eric Clapton
385. Legend: Get Up Stand Up—Bob Marley
386. Kraftwerk: Trans Europe Express
387. Rap cassette: Rappers Delight 1979
388. Run DMC Greatest Hits: Sucker MC's (Krush Groove) 1983
389. Run DMC Greatest Hits: Walk This Way
390. It Takes A Nation Of Millions: Bring The Noise—Public Enemy
391. As Nasty As The Wanna Be: Me So Horny—2 Live Crew 1989
392. Of Ska: Nuclear Weapon—The Skatalites
393. Skampilation cassette: Israelites-Desmond Dekker 1969
394. Legend: I Shot The Sheriff—Bob Marley 1973
395. Hip Hop Classics: F*** The Police—NWA 1988
396. Hip Hop Classics: Push It—Salt N' Peppa 1987
397. Cassette: What You Gonna Do—Puff Daddy
398. Prose Combat: Relations Humaines—MC Solar 1993

Fourteen: MTV

399. Thriller: Billy Jean—Michael Jackson 1982
400. Thriller: Beat It—Michael Jackson 1982
401. Thriller: The Girl Is Mine—Michael Jackson 1982
402. Thriller: Wanna Be—Michael Jackson 1982
403. The Hits 2: I Wanna Be Your Lover—Prince 1978
404. The Hits 2: Purple Rain—Prince 1984
405. True Blue: Papa Don't Preach—Madonna
406. Bruce Springsteen Greatest Hits: Born To Run 1975
407. Bruce Springsteen Greatest Hits: Hungry Heart 1975
408. Bruce Springsteen Greatest Hits: Born In The USA 1984
409. Joshua Tree: Mothers Of The Disappeared—U2

410. Synchro System: Synchro Feelings—Sunny Ade 1983
411. The Guide: Old Man- Youssou N'Dour 1994
412. Graceland: You Can Call Me Al—Paul Simon 1986
413. Graceland: Graceland—Paul Simon 1986
414. Graceland: Homeless—Paul Simon 1986
415. Graceland: I Know What I Know—Paul Simon 1986
416. Graceland: Under African Skies—Paul Simon 1986

Fifteen: Alternative

417. Candy Apple Grey: Crystal—Husker Du 1986
418. Nevermind: Smells Like Teen Spirit—Nirvana 1991
419. Pearl Jam: Alive 1991
420. Loveless: To Here Knows Where—My Bloody Valentine 1991
421. Psychocandy: The Living End—Jesus and Mary Chain 1985
422. Blue Bell Knoll: Blue Bell Knoll—Cocteau Twins 1988
423. Into The Labyrinth: Saldek—Dead Can Dance 1993
424. Daydream Nation: Candle—Sonic Youth 1988
425. Rave: James Brown Is Dead—LA Style 1993
426. The Downward Spiral: Mr Self Destruct—Nine Inch Nails 1994
427. Phish: Wolfman's Brother

Rock and Roll Hall of Fame Inductees

Leaders in the music industry joined together in 1983 to establish the Rock and Roll Hall of Fame Foundation. One of the Foundation's many functions is to recognize the contributions of those who have had a significant impact on the evolution, development and perpetuation of rock and roll by inducting them into the Hall of Fame.

There are four categories of inducteees:

Performers

Artists become elibible for induction 25 years after the release of their first record. Criteria include the influence and significance of the artists contributions to the development and perpetuation of rock and roll.

The Foundation's nominating committee, composed of rock and roll historians, selects nominees each year in the Performer category. Ballots are then sent to an international voting body of about 1,000 rock experts. Those performers who receive the highest number of votes, and more than 50 percent of the vote, are inducted. The Foundation generally inducts five to seven performers each year.

Non-Performers

Songwriters, producers, disc jockeys, record executives, journalists and other industry professionals who have had a major influence on the development of rock and roll.

Early Influences

Artists whose music predated rock and roll but had an impact on the evolution of rock and roll and inspired rock's leading artists.

A special selection committee elects the inductees in the Non-performer and Early Influences categories.

Side Men

This category was introduced in 2000. It honors those musicians who have spent their career out of the spotlight, performing as backup musicians for major artists on recording sessions and in concert. Though they often play a key role in the creation of memorable music, the public rarely knows them by name. A separate committee, composed primarily of producers, selects the inductees in this category.

1986
Chuck Berry
James Brown
Ray Charles
Sam Cooke
Fats Domino
The Everly Brothers
Buddy Holly
Jerry Lee Lewis
Elvis Presley
Little Richard

Non-Performers
Alan Freed
Sam Phillips
Early Influences
Robert Johnson
Jimmie Rodgers
Jimmy Yancey
Lifetime Achievement
John Hammond

1987
The Coasters
Eddie Cochran
Bo Diddley
Aretha Franklin
Marvin Gaye
Bill Haley
B.B. King
Clyde McPhatter
Rick Nelson
Roy Orbison
Carl Perkins
Smokey Robinson
Big Joe Turner
Muddy Waters
Jackie Wilson
Non-Perofrmers
Leonard Chess
Ahmet Ertegun
Jerry Lieber and Mike Stoller
Jerry Wexler
Early Influences
Louis Jordan
T-Bone Walker
Hank Williams

1988
The Beach Boys
The Beatles
The Drifters
Bob Dylan
The Supremes
Non-Performer
Berry Gordy
Early Influences
Woody Guthrie
Leadbelly
Les Paul

1989
Dion
Otis Redding
The Rolling Stones
The Temptations
Stevie Wonder
Non-Performer
Phil Spector
Early Influences
The Ink Spots
Bessie Smith
The Soul Stirrers

1990
Hank Ballard
Bobby Darin
The Four Seasons
The Four Tops
The Kinks
The Platters
Simon and Garfunkel
The Who
Non-Performers
Gerry Goffin and Carole King
Holland, Dozier and Holland
Early Influences
Louis Armstrong
Charlie Christian
Ma Rainey

1991
LaVern Baker
The Byrds
John Lee Hooker
The Impressions
Wilson Pickett
Jimmy Reed
Ike and Tina Turner
Non-Performers
Dave Bartholomew
Ralph Bass
Early Influence
Howlin' Wolf
Lifetime Achievement
Nesuhi Ertegun

1992
Bobby Bland
Booker T. and the MGs
Johnny Cash

Jimi Hendrix Experience
Isley Brothers
Sam and Dave
The Yardbirds
Non-Performers
Leo Fender
Bill Graham
Doc Pomus
Early Influences
Elmore James
Professor Longhair

1993
Ruth Brown
Cream
Creedence Clearwater Revival
The Doors
Etta James
Frankie Lymon and the Teenagers
Van Morrison
Sly and the Family Stone
Non-Performers
Dick Clark
Milt Gabler
Early Influence
Dinah Washington

1994
The Animals
The Band
Duane Eddy
The Grateful Dead
Elton John
John Lennon
Bob Marley
Rod Stewart
Non-Performer
Johnny Otis
Early Influence
Willie Dixon

1995
The Allman Brothers Band
Al Green
Janis Joplin
Led Zeppelin
Martha and the Vandellas
Neil Young
Frank Zappa

Non-Performer
Paul Ackerman
Early Influence
The Orioles

1996
David Bowie
Jefferson Airplane
Gladys Knight and the Pips
Little Willie John
Pink Floyd
The Shirelles
The Velvet Underground
Non-Performer
Tom Donahue
Early Influence
Pete Seeger

1997
Bee Gees
Buffalo Springfield
Crosby, Stills & Nash
Jackson 5
Joni Mitchell
Parliament-Funkadelic
The (Young) Rascals
Non-Performer
Sydney Nathan
Early Influences
Bill Monroe
Mahalia Jackson

1993
The Eagles
Fleetwood Mac
The Mamas and the Papas
Lloyd Price
Gene Vincent
Santana
Non-Performer
Allen Toussaint
Early Influence
Jelly Roll Morton

1999
Billy Joel
Curtis Mayfield
Paul McCartney
Del Shannon
Dusty Springfield

Bruce Springsteen
The Staple Singers
Non-Performer
George Martin
Early Influences
Bob Wills and His Texas Playboys
Charles Brown

2000
Eric Clapton
Earth Wind & Fire
Lovin' Spoonful
The Moonglows
Bonnie Raitt
James Taylor
Non-Performer
Clive Davis
Early Influences
Nat "King" Cole
Billie Holiday
Side Men
King Curtis
James Jamerson
Earl Palmer
Hal Blaine
Scotty Moore

Bibliography

The following are some of the texts consulted in writing this book:

Bacon, Tony, Ed., *Rock Hardware*. New York: Harmony Books, 1981.

Bayles, Martha, *Hole In Our Soul, The Loss Of Beauty And Meaning In American Popular Music*. New York: Free Press, 1994.

Carr, Patrick, ed., *The Illustrated History of Country Music*. New York: Doubleday & Co., 1979.

Charlton, Katherine, *Rock Music Styles, A History*, Second Edition. Madison: Wm. C. Brown, 1993.

Coolidge, Clark, *Now Its Jazz, Writings on Kerouac and the Sounds*. Living Batch Press, 1999.

Corbett, John, *Extended Play: Sounding Off from John Cage To Dr. Funkenstein*. Duke Univ. Press, 1994.

Coupland, Douglas, *Generation X: Tales For An Accelerated Culture*. New York: St. Martin's Press, 1991.

Davis, Stephen, *Hammer Of The Gods: The Led Zeppelin Saga*. New York: Ballantine, 1985.

Derough, Prince, *Popular Music Culture In America*. New York: Ardsley House, 1992.

Epstein, Jonathon, ed., *Adolescents And Their Music*. New York: Garland, 1994.

Felder, Rachel, *Manic Pop Thrill*. Hopewell: Ecco Press, 1993.

Foege, Alec, *Confusion Next: The Sonic Youth Story*. St. Martins' Press, 1994.

Friedlander, Paul, *Rock and Roll, A Social History*. Boulder: Westview, 1996.

George, Nelson, *The Death of Rhythm and Blues*. New York: Pantheon, 1988.

George, Nelson, *Buppies, B-Boys, Baps and Bohos*. New York: Harper and Collins, 1992.

George-Warren, Holly ed., *The Rolling Stone Boof Of The Beats*, Rolling Stone, 1999

Guralnick, Peter, *Last Train To Memphis, The Rise Of Elvis Presley*. Boston: Little, Brown, and Co., 1994.

Hertsgaard, Mark, *A Day In The Life*. New York: Delacorte, 1995.

Hoban, Phoebe, *Basquiat, A Quick Killing In Art*. Viking, 1998

Hirshey, Gerri, *Nowhere To Run, The Story Of Soul Music*. Harrisonburg: R.R.Donnelly, 1985.

Jerzer, Marty, *The Dark Ages: Life In The United States 1945-1960*. Boston: South End Press, 1982.

Jones, Leroi, *Blues People*. New York: Morrow, 1963.

Keil, Charles, *Urban Blues*. Chicago: University of Chicago Press, 1966.

Laing, Dave, *One Chord Wonders, Power And Meaning In Punk Rock*. Philadelphia: Open University Press, 1985.

Manzarek, Ray, *Light My Fire: My Life With The Doors*. P.P.Putnam's Sons,1998

Marsh, Dave, *Before I Get Old: The Story Of The Who*. St. Martin" Press,1983

Miller, Jim, ed. *The Rolling Stone Illustrated History Of Rock and Roll*. New York: Random House, 1976.

O'Grady, Terence, *The Beatles, A Musical Evolution*. Boston: Twayne, 1983.

Pattison, Robert, *The Triumph OF Vulgarity: Rock Music In The Mirror Of Romanticism*. New York: Oxford University Press, 1987.

Riley, Tim, *Hard Rain, A Dylan Commentary*. New York: Borzoi, 1992.

Riley, Tim, *Tell Me Why*. New York: Alfred Knopf, 1988.

Szatmary, David, *Rockin' In Time*, Third Edition. Upper Saddle River: Prentice Hall, 1996.

Thompson, Dave, *Never Fade Away, The Kurt Cobain Story*. New York: St, Martin's Press, 1994.

Tytell, John, *Naked Angels*. New York: Grove Press, 1976.

Ward, Ed., Stokes, Geoffrey, and Tucker, Ken, *Rock Of Ages*. Englewood Cliffs: Prentice Hall, 1986.

Watson, Ben, *Frank Zappa: The Negative Dialectics of Poodle Play*. St. Martins' Press, 1993.

Watson, Steven, *The Birth Of The Beat Generation*. Pantheon, 1995.

White, Timothy, *The Nearest Faraway Place: Brian Wlson, The Beach Boys and the Southern California Experience*. Henry Holt, 1994

Wolfe, Tom, *The Electric Kool-Aid Acid Test*. New York: Farrar, 1968.

Wurtzel, Elizabeth, *Prozac Nation, Young And Depressed In America*. New York: Riverhead Books, 1994.

INDEX

Blind Faith, 48
Blondie, 85
Blood, Sweat, and Tears, 70
Bloomfield, Mike, 70
Blue Flames, The, 56
Blue Grass Boys, The, 10
Bluegrass, 6
Blue Notes, The, 32
Blues Brothers, The, 31
Bolan, Marc, 78
Bon Jovi, 77, 96
Bonham, John, 75-76
Bono, 98
Booker T, 31, 59, 71
Booker T and the MGs, 59
Boone, Pat, 23
Bowie, David, 77, 78, 84, 92, 96
Bracken, James, 4
Bracken, Vivian, 4
Brando, Marlon, 14
Branston, Jackie, 3
Brecker, Michael, 33
Brill Building, 23, 63
British Guitar Bands, 107
British Metal Phase One, 76
British Metal Phase Two, 76
British New Wave, 86
British Punk, 85
British theatrical rock bands, 78
Broonzy, Big Bill, 3
Brown, James, 27, 32, 33, 34, 67, 68, 92
Bruce, Jack, 48, 75
Bruce, Lennie, 37
Bryant, Boudleaux, 18
Bryant, Felice, 18
Buck, Peter, 105
Buffalo Springfield, 62
Burdon, Eric, 48
Burgess, Anthony, 40, 85
Burke, Solomon, 31
Burroughs, William S. , 52
Bush, George, 101
Butler, Jerry, 32
Butterfield, Paul, 36
Byrds, The, 62
Byrne, David, 86, 99

C

Cabaret Voltaire, 107
Cage, John, 83
Cale, J.J. , 49
Cale, John, 83, 84, 86
California Hardcore Punk, 104

California Metal, 77
Cambell, Clive, 91
Cars, The, 84, 86
Carter Family, 10
Carter, A.P. , 10
Carter, Maybelle, 10
Carter, Ron, 70
Carter, Sara, 10
Casale, Jerry, 86
Casey, Harry, 79
Cash, Johnny, 15, 17
Cassidy, Neal, 52
Castaneda, Carlos, 53
Catherine Wheel, 106
Cervenka, Doe, 85
Cervenka, Exene, 85
Chantays, The, 25
Chapman, Tony, 45
Chapman, Tracy, 99
Charles, Ray, 4, 6, 31
Charlie Daniels Band, 63
Checker, Chubby, 22
Chess Bros., 4
Chicago, 70
Chicago Transit Authority, 70
Chords, 6
Christian, Charlie, 59
Chuck D, 92
Chudd, Lew, 4
Ciccone, Madonna Lousie, 97
Clapton, Eric 3, 48-49, 63, 75
Clark, Dave, 3
Clark, Dick, 22-23
Clark, Petulia, 40
Clark, Steve, 76
Clarke, Michael, 62
Clash, 85
Clayton, Adam, 98
Cliff, Jimmy, 69
Cline, Patsy, 11
Clinton, Bill, 93, 101
Clinton, George, 68, 79
Coasters, The, 6, 24
Cobain, Kurt, 106
Cobham, Billy, 70
Cocteau Twins, 107
Collie, Gregg, 54
Collins, Bootsie, 33, 68
Collins, Catfish, 33
Coltrane, John, 57
Columbia Records, 4, 18
Comets, The, 14, 15
Cook, Paul, 85
Cooke, Sam, 6, 31
Cooper, Alice, 79

Cooper, Jack, 4
Copeland, Stewart, 86
Corea, Chick, 70-71
Costello, Elvis, 86
Council, Floyd, 49
Country Joe and the Fish, 54
Country music, 9
Country/Southern Rock, 63
Cox, Billy, Hendrix, 57
Cramer, Floyd, 11, 18
Cream, 48, 75
Creedence Clearwater Revival, 63
Crimson, King, 50
Cropper, Steve, 31
Crosby, Bing, 10
Crosby, David, 62
Crosby, Stills, Nash and Young, 61-62
Crowley, Aleister, 75
Crystals, 24
Curtis, King, 56

D

Daddy-O-Daylie, 14
Dale, Dick, 25
Dali, Salvidore, 83
Daltry, Roger, 47
Danielson, Ellas, 5
Danko, Rich, 63
Dave Clark 5, 40
Dave Matthews Band, 107
David, Hal, 24
Davies, Dave, 49
Davies, Ray, 49
Davis, Miles, 70
Davis, Richard, 65
De Fries, Tony, 78
De Kooning, Willem, 83
De La Soul, 93
Dead Can Dance, 107
Dead Kennedys, 85, 101, 104
Dean, James, 14
Decca Records, 3, 15, 18
Decline of Rock and Roll, 18
Deep Purple, 74, 76
Def Leppard, 76
DeJohnette, Jack, 70
Dekker, Desmond, 91
Delmore Bros. , 10
Densmore, John, 55
Derek and the Dominos, 49
Devo, 86, 96
Dick, Philip K. , 104
Dictators, 84

Diddley, Bo, 4, 5, 47, 59
Dillon, Bob, 36
Dinosaur Jr., 107
Dixon, "Evil" Willie, 3, 49
Domino, Antoine (Fats) , 4
Donegan, Lonnie, 40
Doors, 55
Dozier, Lamont, 29
Dr. Daddy-O, 4
Dr. Hep Cat, 4
Drifters, 4, 6, 24
Drifting Cowboys, 10
Du Champ, Marcel, 83
Dunn, Duck, 31, 59
Duran Duran, 96
Durst, Lavada, 4
Dwight, Reginald Kenneth, 78
Dylan, Bob, 17, 35, 36, 49, 56, 61-63, 65, 77, 99, 17

E

Eagles, The, 63
Earth, Wind and Fire, 69
Eddy, Duane, 25
Edge, The, 98
Electic Flag, 70
Electric guitar, 59
Electric Light Orchestra, The, 50
Emerson, Keith, 71
Emerson, Lake, and Palmer, 50
Eno, Brian, 78, 84, 98
Entwistle, John, 47
Epstein, Brian, 42
Ernst, Max, 83
Ertegun, Ahmet, 4
Etheipian Benefit Concert, 100
European Art Movements, 83
European disco (Eurodisco), 79
Eurythmic, 96
Evans, Bill, 70
Evans, David, 98
Everly Bros., 18, 37

F

Fabian, 22
Fagan, Donald, 70
Fall, The, 107
Fallon, Michael, 52
Farm Aid Benefit concerts, 100
Farrell, Joe, 33
Felder, Don, 63

Fender, Leo, 59
Ferlinghetti, Lawrence, 52
Ferry, Bryan, 78
Field, Marc, 78
Finch, Richard, 79
Fishbone, 69
Fishman, Jan, 107
Flatt, Lester, 10
Flavor Flav, 101
Fleetwood Mac, 66
Fleetwood, Mick, 48
Fogerty, John, 63
Fogerty, Tom, 63
Folk, x, 22
Folk Rock, viii, 62
Folk Song revival, 36
Fonda, Jane, 96
Forte, Fabian, 22
Four Freshmen, The, 25, 26
Four Tops, The, 30
Fournier, Vincent, 79
Frampton, Peter, 66
Francis, Connie, 23
Franklin, Aretha, 27, 31
Frantz, Chris, 86
Fraser, Elizabeth, 107
Freed, Alan, 14, 15, 19
Frey, Glenn, 63
Full Tilt Boogie Band, 56
Funicello, Annette, 25
Funk, viii
Funk and Jazz Rock, 67
Funk Bros., 29

G

Gabriel, Peter, 99
Gale, Mona, 17
Gamble, Kenny, 31-32
Garcia, Jerry, 54, 62
Garfunkel, Art, 37-38
Garland, Judy, 55
Gaye, Marvin, 29, 31
Generation X, 103
Genesis, 99
Gerry and the Pacemakers, 40
Gibb, Barry, 79
Gibb, Maurice, 79
Gibb, Robin, 79

Gibson, Jack, 4
Gilmour, David, 49
Ginsberg, Allen, 37, 52
Girl groups, 24
Glam, 73
Glam/Glitter, ix, 74, 77, 75
Glass, Philip, 86
Gleason, Jackie, 15
Goddard, Stewart, 86
Goffin, Gerry, 23
Golding, William, 40
Gordon, Kim, 104
Gordon, Mike, 107
Gordy, Berry, 29
Gospel, viii, 28
Graham, Bill, 53
Grand Funk Railroad, 77
Grand Ole Opry, 10
Grandmaster Flash, 91, 92
Grateful Dead, 54, 99, 107
Grebo, 106
Greenfield, Howie, 23
Gregory, Dick, 37
Grossman, Steve, 70
Guercio, James, 70
Guiffre, Jimmy, 65
Guns N' roses, 77
Guthrie, Arlo, 38
Guthrie, Woody, 9, 36, 38

H

Hagar, Sammy, 77
Haley, Alex, 69
Haley, Bill, 14-16, 25, 36
Hall, Dusty, 63
Hammer, 93
Hammer, M.C. , 93
Hammond, John, 36, 97
Hammond, Laurene, 71
Hampton, Lionel, 3
Hancock, Herbie, 70, 71
Hard Rock, ix, 74
Hard Rock forerunners, 75
Hard Rock/Heavy Metal, ix
Harris, Oren, 19
Harrison, George, 24, 42, 49, 59, 99
Harry, Debbie, 85
Hart, Billy, 99

Band/Concert Review

Name_____
(attach ticket stub if paid concert, program if free concert)

Name of Band:

Date of Performance:

Location of Performance:

Instrumentation:

Titles of some tunes played (if announced):

Musical style(s) represented:

List specific techniques used:

Write a short essay describing your reactions to the music. Some topics you might comment on could include the quality (tightness or lack thereof) of the ensemble playing, the quality of the soloists and the influences they seem to suggest, and the comprehensibility and impact of the lyrics. Any visual or theatrical elements should also be discussed. Write as much as you can. Use the back if necessary.

Band/Concert Review

Name_____
(attach ticket stub if paid concert, program if free concert)

Name of Band:

Date of Performance:

Location of Performance:

Instrumentation:

Titles of some tunes played (if announced):

Musical style(s) represented:

List specific techniques used:

Write a short essay describing your reactions to the music. Some topics you might comment on could include the quality (tightness or lack thereof) of the ensemble playing, the quality of the soloists and the influences they seem to suggest, and the comprehensibility and impact of the lyrics. Any visual or theatrical elements should also be discussed. Write as much as you can. Use the back if necessary.

Band/Concert Review

Name_____
(attach ticket stub if paid concert, program if free concert)

Name of Band:

Date of Performance:

Location of Performance:

Instrumentation:

Titles of some tunes played (if announced):

Musical style(s) represented:

List specific techniques used:

Write a short essay describing your reactions to the music. Some topics you might comment on could include the quality (tightness or lack thereof) of the ensemble playing, the quality of the soloists and the influences they seem to suggest, and the comprehensibility and impact of the lyrics. Any visual or theatrical elements should also be discussed. Write as much as you can. Use the back if necessary.

Band/Concert Review

Name_____

(attach ticket stub if paid concert, program if free concert)

Name of Band:

Date of Performance:

Location of Performance:

Instrumentation:

Titles of some tunes played (if announced):

Musical style(s) represented:

List specific techniques used:

Write a short essay describing your reactions to the music. Some topics you might comment on could include the quality (tightness or lack thereof) of the ensemble playing, the quality of the soloists and the influences they seem to suggest, and the comprehensibility and impact of the lyrics. Any visual or theatrical elements should also be discussed. Write as much as you can. Use the back if necessary.